The Volkswagen *Beetle*

The Volkswagen *Beetle*

David Hodges

CRESCENT
BOOKS
New York • Avenel

This 1997 edition is published by Crescent Books, a division of Random House Value Publishing, Inc., 40 Engelhard Avenue, Avenel, New Jersey 07001.

Crescent Books and colophon are trademarks of Random House Value Publishing, Inc.

Random House
New York • Toronto • London • Syndey • Auckland
http://www.randomhouse.com/

Printed and Bound in China

A CIP catalog record for this book is available from the Library of Congress

ISBN 0-517-18474-5

8 7 6 5 4 3 2 1

Acknowledgements

The Publisher wishes to thank the photographers who contributed to this book, and to the organizations which made photographs available: Bay View Books, Neill Bruce and The Peter Roberts Collection, Brian Foley, Nick Georgano, Haymarket Motoring Archives, David Hodges, H.J. Klersky, Andrew Morland, The National Motor Museum, Colin Taylor and Volkswagen (UK).

PRECEDING PAGES

An early 'oval window' Beetle from the middle of the 20th century, and (RIGHT) a new Beetle for the end of the century.

BELOW

The North Bay Line runs for hundreds of miles through Northern Ontario, surviving as a public service for a few isolated communities and hydro-electric schemes. A lightweight vehicle for maintenance crews made more sense than a full-blown train for this purpose in the Seventies, hence this delightful Beetle and caravan equipage.

CONTENTS

INTRODUCTION

The people's car – generically, *volkswagen* in German – is almost as old as the automobile, and the type was familiar in Germany long before the advent of the Volkswagen. Usually these 'popular' cars were minimal cars, though size and simplicity did not necessarily bring them within the reach of the ordinary man in the street.

Henry Ford did build a successful universal car, to sell at a low price, but his Model T with its 2.9-litre engine was by no means a small car, nor

was the Model A that followed it. When it was in production in the late 1920s, small 'proper' cars in Germany ranged from the 700-cc DKW to the 1-litre Opel, with small Adlers, the BMW Dixi (a licence-built Austin Seven) and the NSU-Fiats to come. These stimulated desire rather than demand, as the simple DKW cost more than a year's wage for an average worker. This prompted motorcycle manufacturer Zündapp to commission a low-cost car design from Dr Ferdinand Porsche's new design studio. The

project did not get far, but a Porsche-designed NSU that reached the prototype stage in 1933 accurately foreshadowed the Volkswagen.

The idea of a people's car appealed to Porsche, and it fascinated Adolf Hitler. When the Nazi Party came to power in 1933, one of his pet notions was the concept of motoring for the masses, and a meeting with Porsche was to be a meeting of minds. Once again Porsche was commissioned to design a popular car, and when the first ludicrously tight financial limits were relaxed he accepted the technical challenge.

It is possible that Porsche received too much credit for the design of the Volkswagen, for most of the technical elements had been seen before in the work of such men as Ledwinka, Rumpler, Rabe and Nibel. The Volkswagen reflected the Porsche Büro's earlier designs, but it was to reach production and eventually succeed beyond the wildest limits of the Thirties dream.

It was an original concept on the whole: cheap and simple in terms of construction, light in weight to compensate for modest engine performance, with features that met demanding cost limitations. By the standards of the Thirties it was a full-size car, and it is only in North America that it could ever have been regarded as a small car. The first hand-built prototypes were completed in 1935 and, with three more built in 1936, were carefully tested and analyzed by the *Reichsverband der Deutschen Automobilindustrie* (RDA), the German Auto Industry Association, and its report was generally favourable. There were misgivings concerning the target price, but these failed to take into account that production was intended to be at a rate never before achieved in Europe and that there was to be State funding. Other companies were unimpressed, and lost no opportunity to snipe at the project.

Further prototypes were built by Mercedes-Benz and body builder Reutter in 1937, before the design was frozen in 1938 – the pre-production phase was long. These early cars were extensively tested and demonstrated in Germany, for these were to be cars for German workers.

In 1938 work started on a plant to be dedicated to the production of the KdF-Wagen, as Hitler had decreed the car should be known – *Kraft durch Freude* (Strength through Joy). It was to be sold through a savings scheme, and Germans bought stamps on into 1940, having proved their Aryan suitability to own a classless car.

Production was sluggish before the Second World War, but through to 1944 some 640

Ferdinand Porsche, 'father of the Beetle', *with one of the VW38 pre-production cars during tests in 1939. This is a* cabriolimousine, *with roll-back canvas roof.*

saloons were built, alongside larger numbers of military derivatives. This activity ceased when the incomplete and under-utilized factory was largely destroyed in USAF air raids in 1944, being a legitimate target because of its involvement with aircraft parts and repair work, and the production of military vehicles.

Its recovery very soon after the end of the war was largely due to British efforts, although production of the Volkswagen was on a hand-to-mouth basis and therefore naturally limited. Reports by Allied experts were unflattering, and German fears that Volkswagen might be seized by one of the victorious powers began to fade. In January 1948 Heinrich (Heinz) Nordhoff was appointed by the British to run the enterprise. He was sceptical: *'The Volkswagen was anything but a beauty. It was badly sprung, with mediocre*

brakes, badly equipped and upholstered, noisy
and hard-riding. Above all, its engine had no
durability. But its designer had worked something
into it that made this rough diamond very much
worth our while to polish.'

Nordhoff did not permit odd spin-off
products to deflect Volkswagen from its basic
one-model saloon car policy which was to be
successful beyond imagination, production

booming through the Fifties as the Beetle
achieved world-wide sales. It was first dubbed
Käfer in Germany, the name being used as early
as 1942 and appearing as *Beetle* in British
motoring magazines soon after the end of the
Second World War. It became known as the
'Bug' in North America, *Coccinelle* (lady bird)
in France, while the Italians knew it as the
Maggiolino (May bug is a reasonable translation,

and perhaps the most apt. VW lore has it that Ferdinand Porsche set out to design a car 'as streamlined as a May bug').

Like Ford's Model T, the Beetle eventually outlived its sell-by date, at least in countries in the automotive mainstream (it went on and on in other regions). The millionth Beetle was completed in August 1955, the 10-millionth in November 1967, the 20-millionth was built in Mexico in 1982. Early in 1972 the Volkswagen took the production record from the Model T – the perspective of the vastly larger potential market is sometimes overlooked – then as Ford revised its total, the 'score' was put beyond dispute in 1973 when Beetle production exceeded 16,561,850.

The distinctive car had been a key feature of the West German economic miracle – Volkswagenwerk was one of the country's largest customers for raw materials, and its largest exporter in the Fifties. Its sales and service network spread across the world, and Beetles were built, or assembled from CKD kits, in countries from Nigeria to Peru, South Africa to Australia, Ireland to the Far East. Volkswagen do Brasil and Volkswagen de Mexico became important companies, and in the mid-Nineties were still building Beetles.

Factory fresh in 1996 – a brand-new Beetle outside the Puebla plant in Mexico.

Along the way, sales of the Beetle had soared in America, where so many imports had flopped, where the car was highly unconventional, and on

the face of it, plain unsuitable among the generally large and floppy cars of the Fifties and even the down-sized models of the Sixties. The image created by award-winning advertising campaigns helped, the Bug customizing craze that spread from the West Coast helped, sporty derivatives helped, but respected commentator on the automotive scene, Henry Manney, possibly put a finger on a prime reason for its success when he discussed automobile choice in California in 1971: *'Perhaps all VW owners round here are nearest to the truth ... VWs are much more appropriate here than in their homeland where a high degree of acceleration and good wet-weather roadholding are at a premium.'*

The master mind responsible for the Volkswagen's most impressive growth, Heinrich Nordhoff, died in the spring of 1968, and company expansion changed direction as Auto Union and NSU were acquired. The Beetle was difficult to replace, but as sales fell in most

Concept I, which was to be the basis of the New Beetle design, posed with an original Beetle in 1994.

markets in the early Seventies, Volkswagenwerk AG was forced to replace it. A true successor to this car, with its air-cooled engine mounted at the rear, came in the form of the front-wheel-drive, water-cooled Golf in 1974: three years later, European Beetle production was being run down, and in 1978 the last – Karmann convertibles – were sold.

However, the Beetle story did not end in Europe in the Seventies, or in Latin America in the Nineties. The image of the car was one of the strongest in the history of motoring, and it refused to fade as the numbers of Beetles on public roads inevitably began to decline. The cars in Volkswagen's ranges in the Nineties were competent, but none was distinctive in the way the Beetle was. That hurt sales, especially in the United States where VW sales fell below 50,000 in 1993. Therefore, VW-Audi chose to unveil a retro-style concept car, with surface shapes strongly reminiscent of the Beetle, at the Detroit Show early in 1994. The instant reaction from

possible buyers – who saw it as a 'new Beetle' or 'Beetle II' – was so positive that VW-Audi just had to develop it as a production model. As the new Beetle, a development was exhibited in 1996, and with it came the understanding that it would be in showrooms by 1998. That is a remarkable tribute to the classic Beetle.

When the end came in Europe, the original Beetle had been around for more than four decades and had been steadily developed for 30 years since true production began. That is the main theme of this book, the story of a quite remarkable machine and more than half a century of accomplishment, of a car that achieved cult status and more than fulfilled its original motoring-for-the masses objective.

1. THE PEOPLE'S CAR

Forerunners of the Beetle, the Porsche Type 12 (ABOVE) built for Zündapp, photographed outside Porsche's house in 1932, and (OPPOSITE) the Type 32 built for NSU in 1934. This Type 32 is the only surviving Porsche 'pre-Beetle' prototype. It has a steel body by Drauz, whereas the other two Type 32s had Reutter fabric bodies. Its lines clearly anticipate the Beetle.

The origins of the Beetle design initially stemmed from the Porsche Büro in Stuttgart. Ferdinand Porsche had set up the design studio when he left Steyr in 1930 as that famous old Austrian firm was taken over by Austro-Daimler. Backing came from one-time racing driver Adolf Rosenberger, and Porsche's first lieutenants were Austrian – Karl Rabe, Karl Fröhlich, Josef Zahradnik, Josef Kales, and soon Erwin Komenda, covering the automotive engineering spectrum. The term Porsche Büro, incidentally, is generally used as a handy simplification of an enormously ponderous, all-embracing company title.

The Büro's first designs – numbered 7 and 8, to give clients the impression of a 'back list' – were for Wanderer, a company soon to become part of the Auto Union combine.

In 1931, the Porsche independent front suspension was patented. It interested many manufacturers, and was to be important to the

Volkswagen. It was devised around torsion bars, not new as such, but in this arrangement the two transverse bars were housed in a tubular cross member, with a lower trailing link at each end, and an upper link pivoted to the frame and combined with a friction shock absorber. This was lighter than the then-common transverse leaf spring arrangement, but it meant that the wheels rolled with the body.

Work soon began on a small rear-engined car for Zündapp, and the prototype emerged as a neat two-door saloon, with a 'streamlined' tail. The rear-mounted engine was a Zündapp water-cooled 1.2-litre five-cylinder radial unit, specified by the motorcycle manufacturer and hardly a sound idea! The project was dropped as Fritz Neumeyer of Zündapp decided to concentrate on what his company knew best – the manufacture of motorcycles.

At the same time, the little Standard Superior designed by Josef Ganz was prepared for modest and short-lived production at a small factory at Ludwigsburg. This constitutes an interesting fragment of motoring history as it had independent suspension all round, a backbone chassis, engine ahead of the rear axle and aerodynamic bodywork, and it was promoted as a *volkswagen.*

Back in the Porsche mainstream, the Type 32 for NSU came in 1933. This was similar in specification and some aspects of appearance to the Tatra V570 designed by Hans Ledwinka and Erich Ubelacker, which apparently impressed Hitler as much as the Tatra T11 he had used in the Twenties. Be that as it may, the Type 32 can be seen as the direct forerunner of the Volkswagen. It had Porsche's torsion bar front suspension, a rear-mounted 1.5-litre air-cooled engine designed by Kales and body lines that anticipated the Beetle, styled by Komenda. But because of close associations with Fiat, NSU backed away.

The Type 32 was inevitably in the background when Porsche met Hitler in 1933 to discuss the Auto Union Grand Prix car project and so, perhaps, were the Führer's conversations with Ledwinka. Hitler subsequently outlined his theories of a popular car to Porsche. These were not too far removed from the stillborn NSU: the car was to carry five (two adults and three adolescents were shown sprawled out in an artist's sketch prepared for publicity): it was to have an air-cooled engine, and be capable of 100 km/h (62 mph). The selling price was to be 1,000 Reich Marks (then £86), or less, and costings were to assume an annual production rate of 50,000 units. An interesting comparison is the Ford Model Y which the Dagenham company marketed as a 60-mph full four-seater from October 1935, at £100 (or 1,165 RM).

Porsche took on the commission, basing the Type 60 that was to become the Volkswagen on the Type 32. Prototypes were not completed to the first extremely tight deadlines, but two hand-built cars with bodies from outside suppliers were built in the garage of Porsche's Stuttgart house and

were running before the end of 1935. One was a saloon (V1: *versuchs*, or experimental, 1), which outwardly appeared to be at a halfway stage between the NSU and the definitive Beetle shape that was to come two years later. V2 was a cabriolet.

Three VW3 prototypes were then built, with bodies by Daimler-Benz. These exceeded the 650-kg (1,430-lb) target weight by considerable margins. They were to be used in a rushed and extensive test programme, each covering 50,000 km (31,000 miles) in 750-km (466-mile) daily cycles in 1936.

There was a backbone chassis, forked at the rear to mount the engine, and while those first two cars had wooden floors, from the second batch of prototypes the basis was a platform chassis. The torsion bar front suspension was used, and there were torsion bars at the rear, in conjunction with a swing axle layout. This was cheap to make but, coupled with the rearward weight bias, endowed the car with pronounced oversteer and unpredictable cornering habits.

The first cars were to be used as test beds

with various engines. A two-stroke four-cylinder 850-cc unit was tried, and two horizontally-opposed 'boxer' twin-cylinder engines followed, one with sleeve valves, the other with normal overhead valves. Then Fritz Reimspiess outlined a four-cylinder, air-cooled boxer engine; this Type E was costed and designed quickly, and was the type fitted to the second batch of prototypes, then to generations of Beetles.

It had a magnesium crankcase, cast-iron cylinder barrels, and aluminium cylinder heads. A forged crankshaft was soon to replace the cheaper cast-iron item because of persistent failures. The three main bearings were small, the camshaft arrangement for the pushrod overhead valves was simple, the inlet ports were restricted – all features aimed at keeping down costs, but incidentally frustrating to would-be tuners. A large fan was called for, and was to be an irritating source of noise.

In its first 985-cc form, the peak power of 22.5 bhp was developed at 3000 rpm, while at the end of the Thirties, the production unit was to be rated at 25 bhp at 3300 rpm, although this was

actually achieved only when an enlarged engine came in 1943. These output figures may not have been exciting, but the boxer engine was to earn a remarkable reputation for longevity in later years.

Cost considerations meant that the three-speed gearbox did not have synchromesh. The gearing was deliberately high, and that helped to foster the unbreakable reputation that was to come. Grouping engine and transmission at the rear saved weight and complication as a propeller shaft was unnecessary, and of course there were savings as a radiator and coolant plumbing were not needed.

In road performance, good aerodynamics helped, with the flat underside contributing to a drag figure later claimed to be 0.38, but probably no better than 0.4, while the car was light (kerb weight 650 kg/1,430 lb, with a little more put on before it reached production). Contemporaries were most impressed by the willingness of later prototype cars to cruise all day at maximum speed; however, carefully picked drivers were chosen for demonstration runs.

The thirty VW30 prototypes were built by Daimler-Benz and proved unbreakable through the test and development stages. This meant that the purposes of the extended trials were indeed served, for it is reasonable to suspect that as the *Reichsverband der Deutschen Automobilindustrie* (RDA), which was responsible for the programme seemed opposed to the project, its engineers would not spare the prototypes. Eventually, RDA lost out in the factional infighting so typical of a totalitarian state and had to approve the car, at least in its main features.

The entire programme was then taken out of the hands of the German auto industry establishment and was adopted as a State enterprise under the name of *Deutsche Arbeitsfront* (DAF), the labour organization. Testing was then undertaken by members of the SS.

In 1938 the foundation stone of the KdF-Wagen factory was laid (Volkswagenwerk was abruptly dropped) and the town that was to become Wolfsburg was planned. The plant was deliberately situated well away from the heartland of the German automobile industry, roughly halfway between Hanover and

One of the faults of the VW30 was the small opening giving access to the nose compartment, which made spare wheel removal difficult (the lines of the lid can be seen in the shot).

OPPOSITE

In May 1938 Adolf Hitler laid the foundation stone for the Wolfsburg factory in a ceremony inspired by the nationalistic feeling of the time. (ABOVE) He was obviously pleased with the car, trying the rear passenger seats as well as the front. Ferdinand Porsche (standing beside the driver's door) seemed happy at this stage, although during the day it was abruptly announced that the car was to be named the KdF-Wagen, which apparently upset him.

Magdeburg in Lower Saxony, and some of its methods and machinery came from the America, as did skilled workers and executives who had emigrated in the harrowing years of the Twenties.

Nominally, production started in 1939 and publicity – or propaganda – for the car continued through to 1941. Predictably, as Czechoslovakia was invaded by Germany, patent infringement action initiated by Tatra against the KdF-Wagen company was to fail, but after the Second World War some compensation was paid to Tatra's German subsidiary.

The traditional motor trade distribution system was set aside, and DAF ran a savings scheme for would-be buyers. These were vetted, and when approved could buy a weekly stamp, at 5 RM; half of the total purchase price had to be collected in the form of stamps before an order became firm. Many years later, savers were to battle with Volkswagen through local and state courts and eventually at national level until, in 1970, their entitlement to a discount on a new VW, or a modest refund, was established.

There were many detail changes in the final Reutter-built VW38 pre-production batch and some VW39 demonstration cars before the definitive KdF-Wagen (that would become Volkswagen Type 1) appeared. There were doors hinged at the A pillar rather than at the middle; there were small running boards, a fully-opening nose compartment cover hinged at the bulkhead; a revised tail with a split rear window and tidier engine cover – the earlier rear end had been very beetle-like – and there were bumpers.

Two body styles were to be offered, a saloon and a semi-cabriolet with a roll-back cloth roof. The spare wheel and fuel tank were in the nose, the cockpit was spartan, and luggage space was provided between the rear seats and the engine. The seats were comfortable, and the front pair could be adjusted, although only when the car was at rest.

In general, it was not a refined car: in some respects its performance was modest and it was very noisy, but it promised to fulfil the popular transport role foreseen for it.

Simplicity – the definitive KdF-
Wagen chassis, with mechanical
components in place, seats to
clearly define the layout, and a very
crude fuel tank in a position that
later generations would come to
regard as hazardous.

INSET
This cutaway drawing distorts
proportions in a well-established
tradition of automotive brochure
artwork. The happy family of small
people (and the improbable steering
wheel) gave potential buyers an
impression of a spacious interior,
while no Beetle before 1970 could
have accommodated that amount of
luggage in the nose.

Specification **KdF-Wagen**				
Engine:	4 cylinders, horizontally opposed, air-cooled; 70 x 64 mm, 985 cc; 23.5 bhp at 3000 rpm (1938), then 22.5 bhp at 3000 rpm			hydraulic shock absorbers; rear, independent, swing axle, radius arms and torsion bars, hydraulic shock absorbers
Transmission:	Four-speed manual gearbox	**Brakes:**		Drum
Suspension:	Front, independent by torsion bars and trailing arms,	**Dimensions:**		Wheelbase, 94.5 in (240 cm); front track, 51 in (129.5 cm); rear track, 49 in (124.5 cm); weight, 1,433 lb (650 kg)
		Maximum speed:		62 mph (100 km/h) claimed in 1939

2. STARTING FROM ZERO

A bomb-wrecked assembly hall at Wolfsburg in 1944, with a part-completed military Kübelwagen on the right. This gives an accurate impression of the state of the whole plant towards the end of the Second World War, but production got under way remarkably quickly under British supervision.

By the late spring of 1945 Germany was in ruins, and KdF-Stadt fell in the British occupation zone. The factory that was the reason for its existence had been largely destroyed in U.S. Air Force raids in 1944 and names devised in the Nazi era now had to be erased. The embryo town became Wolfsburg, after a nearby castle of that name (some suggested the name change was proposed by the British), while the factory was briefly renamed the Wolfsburg Motor Works, before Volkswagen was adopted.

It was Wolfsburg's good fortune to fall under British Military rule. Presumably, the Soviets at that time would merely have stripped whatever remained of the plant and there seemed to have been little of immediate value or interest to the Americans and the French. But the British needed light transport for their occupation forces and it was only common sense to provide local work. The two considerations dovetailed neatly.

It is easy to assume that the Western Allies could have taken whatever they wished by way of reparations in the following years, but there was an awareness of complicated questions of ownership and future repercussions. Ford looked at this possibility as late as 1948, and the legal aspects apparently worried company executives: Chairman Ernest Breech's famous aside to Henry

Ford II was also discouraging: 'Mr Ford, I don't think what they have got here is worth a damn.' The French motor industry was offended by their government's proposition that Volkswagen should be taken over, and its opposition killed off that possibility. There were British reports on the vehicles, on the saloon to add to experience with captured military derivatives. Humber findings after evaluating one of these were added to a later analysis by Rootes experts and incorporated in a Society of Motor Manufacturers and Traders (SMMT) report published by the British Intelligence Objective Sub-Committee (BIOS) in 1947, under a ponderous title. This praised the body construction, damned the engine and concluded that the car would fail to be attractive to the average potential buyer as *'it is too ugly and too noisy ... it will remain popular for two or three years ... commercially it would be a completely uneconomic enterprise ...'*. By that time it had been in production, under British control, since 1945.

Odd cars were assembled from spares almost as soon as the British arrived, followed by a batch based on the Type 82 Kübelwagen chassis (a military derivative – *see* Chapter 5). Then came the significant appointment of Royal Electrical and Mechanical Engineers Major Ivan Hirst, to govern town and plant, to meet military needs and restart production. This proceeded in primitive conditions, but by the end of 1945 the factory had turned out more than 2,400 saloons and vans. These varied in details as suspected design faults were corrected but it was usual for odd components to be used in a hand-to-mouth operation (the fish-based glue used on the interior panels is often quoted for its overpowering smell in hot weather!)

Most of the saloons comprised Kübelwagen chassis with saloon bodies sitting oddly high above the generous ground clearance and designated Type 51, with just a handful of standard cars. In place of the original designations came Type 11 for the standard saloon, while Type 13 was to have a sliding roof and Type 15 was the convertible. Beyond that, the Kübelwagen became Type 21, while Types 51, 53 and 55 were to be used for Kübelwagen chassis

By 1949 there was a limited choice of colours – the standard Beetle was still black, but red, brown and green paintwork was available on Export cars. (ABOVE) This is a 'split window' car, and a dating detail is the pair of small grilles below the headlights, one for the horn, and the other a dummy (in 1952 oval grilles were introduced). The fascia (LEFT) was simple, with a speedometer optimistically calibrated to 120 km/h (75 mph). Wiper and lights switches were below it, flanking the ignition switch. The starter button is on the centre line, with the turn indicator switch above it (just below the 'screen). This car also has a non-standard windscreen washer plunger. The spare panel carries the optional mechanical clock (late Thirties pre-production cars sometimes had a radio in this position).

with bodies corresponding to 11, 13 and 15. These came about simply because some Kübelwagen chassis were available.

Whatever their designations, these immediate post-war Volkswagens were basic vehicles, but acceptable through a period when a new car of any sort was a rarity. Suspension and body were carried over from the pre-production KdF-Wagen, as much of the tooling survived: so was the air-cooled boxer engine and the transmission,

save that the engine had the larger capacity introduced during the war, when a requirement for more powerful engines for military vehicles led to the unit with an increased bore, that had been tested in 1937-38, being adopted. The enlargement from 985 cc to 1131 cc produced almost 10 per cent more power, to a rating of 24.5 bhp at 3300 rpm (soon rounded up to 25 bhp). There was no top speed improvement, although the quality of materials may have undermined performance for a while – certainly those early post-war engines were not renowned for longevity (careful detail improvement was called for, too, and shortcomings were soon overcome).

During the Second World War the Porsche Büro had proposed turbocharged and supercharged versions of the flat four, and a diesel. A synchromesh gearbox was also put forward, but the old crash 'box was to serve through to 1952.

However, the direct involvement of the Porsche company did not end. Ferdinand Porsche was held by the French from 1945 until 1947 and was consulted during the development of the Renault 4CV, a rear-engined model intended to fill the same role as the Beetle. He returned to Austria to approve the sports car designed by his son, Ferry, the first car of the Porsche marque which used many VW components. The Porsche company was to become a primary Volkswagen R&D consultant, and VW was to pay it a royalty of a few pence on every Beetle built, while Porsche was to design and build numerous prototypes for Volkswagen through to the Eighties. However, Ferdinand Porsche had no further personal involvement in the popular car his Büro had designed in the Thirties.

Meanwhile, VW production just exceeded 10,000 in 1946, but fell back a little in 1947 when the Beetle was exhibited at a show for the first time since 1939. It was then that Volkswagen became Germany's largest car manufacturer by volume as production increased steadily until it reached more than a million in 1965.

By 1947 the British were seeking to withdraw from the enterprise. Eventually, in September 1949, Volkswagenwerk GmbH was handed over to the West German government, very much as a going concern. The British had done more than get production under way and protect the factory, for arguably their most important contribution to the future was in appointing most of the senior executives who were to see VW through to prosperity, above all, the autocratic ex-Opel director Heinrich (Heinz) Nordhoff. The modern company acknowledges its debts to the British, and especially to Yorkshireman Ivan Hirst.

Type 11

Well before the handover, the make-up of the car had been stabilized. Its shape was already familiar, and while the mechanical layout was still unconventional, details like the flat windscreen hinted at the age of the design. The lightly stressed engine brings to mind one Thirties requirement, and others were to be found in economic details such as the cable brakes. The semaphore indicators, which now seem quaint, were actually in line with contemporary practices. Six-volt electrics were to last until 1967 (on U.S. cars – until 1968 on European cars). Importantly, engine reliability was to be improved.

Entry was easy through the wide doors, and very soon their excellent sealing was to attract wide favourable comment, for it was outstanding among 'popular' cars: nevertheless, in motion the body was not as rigid as later unitary-construction types. The front seats were comfortable, and while much was made of rear-seat headroom, less was said about the inadequate leg space. Visibility was good for the driver, by the standards of the day, although the pillars were soon to seem thick.

The fascia was simple, with two open cubby holes in the painted metal, a multi-function round instrument (speedo plus three warning lights) with an optional clock available to give symmetry in the position where pre-Second World War publicity had shown a radio. Oddly, the late-Thirties cars had glove-box covers. There was no fuel gauge, but a visual check was easy through the generous filler neck – a wooden dipstick was offered – and there was a main/reserve fuel tap on the bulkhead beneath the fascia. A thin-rimmed three-spoke steering wheel was standard (a 'superior' two-spoke wheel, white to match the minor control knobs, was optional), and there was a rather spindly central gear lever. The spare wheel and fuel tank took up most of the nose compartment – it had to be opened for access to the fuel filler – but there was room for small pieces of luggage, to supplement the main space behind the rear seats.

The gearbox had to be used frequently if a reasonable speed was to be maintained in traffic, or on winding and hilly roads, but the virtue of uncomplaining cruising at or near the maximum speed was still impressive. The 40/60 weight distribution gave light steering and good traction, but in combination with the swing axles did make for the oversteer qualities that were rightly criticized for years: it paid to be aware of this shortcoming in cross-winds. The ride was bouncy but good by Forties standards, especially when the car was fully laden.

Tested by *The Motor* in June 1947, an 1131-cc Beetle had a top speed of 57.3 mph (92.2 km/h), and 0-50 mph (0-80 km/h) acceleration took 29.4 seconds. In most respects this seemed a

ABOVE

A sectioned mid-Fifties car, showing the reshaped fuel tank (and its filler cap under the nose lid) and the installation of the engine behind the rear wheels, but with its main weight carried low in the chassis.

LEFT

An early 'oval window' Beetle, dating from 1953. The replacement of the split rear window was regarded as a major modification. Otherwise, there was little change in the second post-Second World War generation of Beetles. By modern standards the engine compartment (BELOW) appears uncluttered, and the power unit very straightforward.

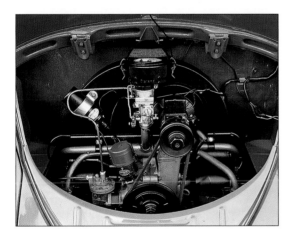

car, but an unlikely candidate for the massive sales and the cult status that was to come.

Developing a Best Seller

The first period, the 'split window' era, lasted until 1953. It saw a continuing programme of modification, largely to details of fittings and trim. Distinguishing items included the grooved bumpers, with little overriders which looked as if they had been fitted backwards, until 1949, before chromed bumpers came; the 'Pope's nose' rear stop light and number plate light housing 1947-52; an internal release for the nose compartment so that the handle became a simple lifting aid, and from 1949 a cable release from the cockpit.

The introduction of the Export model in mid-1949 was significant, for its title recognized the sales potential of the Beetle and the effort that Nordhoff was directing into new markets. The first formal export sales had already been made, to the Netherlands in 1947: by 1948, 23 per cent of Beetle production was exported – 4,464 cars to Belgium, Denmark, Luxembourg, Sweden and Switzerland. Meanwhile, odd cars had been brought into Britain by returning armed forces personnel. Colborne Garages set up a spares service, out of which grew the first VW dealership in Britain, in 1952, when the first right-hand-drive cars were built in Germany; British currency regulations meant that foreign cars could be imported only for sale to foreigners until 1953. Eire had no motor industry of her own and was the site of the first Beetle assembly plant outside Germany: set up by entrepreneur Denis Connolly, this was to assemble some 83,000 Beetles, 1950-68. Other European outlets were soon established, sometimes with dealers in non-competing marques, such as Chrysler: but some European countries took measures to protect their industries and for a while staved off the Beetle invasion.

Nordhoff looked further afield, especially to countries with under-developed road systems, for example in Africa. The first Beetle arrived in South Africa in 1950 and assembly started there the same year, with local content gradually increasing and 'special editions' coming along in the Seventies. Australia was to prove disappointing. Beetles were assembled from 1957, and the large plant that came into operation in 1960 at Clayton, near Melbourne, was expected to match VW's Brazilian operation. Rally success boosted expectations; a government-imposed requirement for an unrealistic local content dashed them. Eventually, the plant was sold to Nissan.

The United States was a prime target for European manufacturers in the post-Second World War years, and many failed. Volkswagen's Dutch importer, Ben Pon, tried to interest Americans in the Beetle in 1949. As the Fifties opened, Hoffman of New York imported a few Beetles – or Bugs – but could really see no future for the car in a pampered market (by mid-decade Hoffman was obviously much happier with Porsche). Nordhoff was nevertheless convinced that there was much more than niche market potential, and Volkswagen of America was set up to explore and exploit that market.

Before that, at the end of the Forties, Nordhoff had visited Brazil, and the first outcome was a modest assembly arrangement. That led to a new factory outside São Paulo, which completed its first vehicle (a Transporter) in 1957 and its first Beetle in 1959. That year it turned out 8,445, and soon it was exporting cars to other Latin American countries as well as kits to be assembled in Nigeria.

The Export model, originating in Germany,

was obviously a de luxe version, and from the outset that meant more than chrome embellishment. There were telescopic shock absorbers at the front, and from the spring of 1951 at the back, too; importantly, hydraulic brakes were introduced in 1950.

That year also saw a fabric sun-roof option, echoing a Thirties variant. As far as the normal body was concerned, a first approach to improving ventilation was the introduction of venting rear windows in 1950-51, then flaps at knee height in the front quarter panels (the 'crotch coolers') were tried for a year before the most obvious solution was adopted – opening quarter lights in the front door windows. The 1952 arrangement incidentally meant that the semaphore turn indicators had to be repositioned in the B pillars. Also, in 1952, synchromesh was added to the top three gear ratios on Export cars, and 16-inch wheels were replaced by 15-inch. Internally, the fascia was restyled, with the speedo positioned directly ahead of the driver so that the cubby hole that had been offset from the boss of the wheel was lost. The glove compartment on the passenger side gained a lid (the cabriolets had a lockable glove box). Among other details, self-cancelling wipers were introduced and there was also an attractive 'Wolfsburg' badge – water and castle surmounted by a wolf – which just lasted out a decade.

LEFT Contemporary side view of a Hebmüller shows off the car's dumpy lines. It is suggested that this version inspired the one-off coupé (BELOW) built by Stoll in 1952. This has a luxurious 2+2 interior, but standard mechanical components. Restoration took owner Bob Shaill many years.

Cabriolets

While Volkswagen undertook production of the Type 2 'family' (Transporter, Kombi, Micro) it left Beetle soft-tops to outside specialists, despite its pre-war open KdF-Wagen and a couple of cars built at Wolfsburg during the rehabilitation period. There were two approved cabriolets, which shared mechanical upratings with the Type 11 saloons, a two-seater built by Hebmüller and a four-seater by the long-established Karmann coachbuilding company.

The Hebmüller cabriolet (Type 14) followed the lines of one of the 1946 cars, Colonel Charles Radclyffe's convertible, devised at Hirst's suggestion (Radclyffe was responsible for light industry in the British zone of Germany, and VW had come under his overall control). Hebmüller's chassis was necessarily reinforced, with a substantial girder on each side, while a sturdy windscreen surround was the main contribution to upper body rigidity. The soft top was effective when erected, but bulky when lowered, so that it took up much of the space behind the seats (although this was a 'two-seater', there was room for two small children or some luggage in the rear). The engine cover was distinguished by an air scoop that gave the impression of a spine. This cabriolet was introduced alongside the Export saloon in 1949, but production was erratic, eventually reaching around 750. By 1953,

however, Hebmüller was bankrupt, and the last of its cabriolets were actually built by Karmann.

That company's conversion (Type 15) had provided stiff competition for Hebmüller, not only because it was a full four-seater, admittedly at the aesthetic cost of the folded soft-top overhanging the engine compartment. Its chassis was similarly strengthened and like the Type 14 it was naturally heavier than the saloon by some 265 lb (120 kg). Its nose followed standard lines, but as the folded soft-top masked the engine air

intakes there were louvres for this purpose in the engine cover (vertical until 1957, then in a neater horizontal arrangement). These cars carried little Karmann badges.

The Karmann conversion was a great success, with a third of a million sold in 31 years – it actually outlived the saloon in production in Europe. Other specialists produced small numbers of open cars on the basis of Beetles, but as these did not have the official status of VW type numbers they are covered among the 'specials' in Chapter 8.

On the Road

In its 1952 form, the saloon with the 1131-cc engine rated at 25 bhp was tested by *The Motor* in Britain and *Road & Track* in the United States, and both magazines achieved closely similar performance figures – a 66-mph (106-km/h) top speed and a 0-50 mph (0-80 km/h) acceleration time of 22.5 seconds. A test by *The Autocar* in 1953 returned fractionally slower figures.

The split rear window era ended in March 1953, and the larger oval window that replaced it was to last until 1967. This feature is not reliable for dating purposes as conversions were possible, and the split rear window may have been reinstated in more recent restorations. However, the introduction of the 1192 cc flat four in 1954 was more important in all respects save easy identification (the bore was increased from 75 mm to 77 mm, while the stroke remained at 64 mm). This '1200' engine was first rated at 30 bhp, at 3400 rpm, and the effect was to increase the maximum speed to 68 mph (109 km/h) when tested by *The Motor*, while *Road & Track*

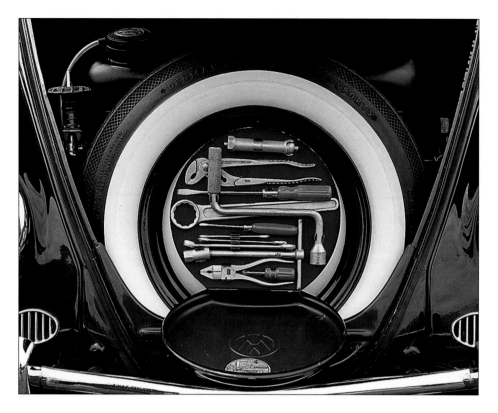

recorded a less impressive improvement, to a 65-mph (105-km/h) top speed.

There was more to come, and with an increased compression ratio and another 300 revs there was a modest power boost for 1955. This led to improvements in almost every aspect of performance, except fuel consumption (poorer by as much as 3 mpg in overall terms). *The Motor* road test in 1956 recorded a mean top speed of 68.2 mph (109.7 km/h), while *Road & Track* recorded 70.2 mph (113 km/h). Respective 0-50 mph (0-80 km/h) acceleration times were 18.2 and 18.0 seconds. This Beetle was also much more flexible, noticeably in top gear, so that the gears had to be used less often to keep up with traffic flow.

Those 1955 cars had a little more room for rear-seat passengers, and more for luggage (the rear seat cushion could also be removed and the seat back folded down to give a large flat space). There was more free space in the nose, too, as the fuel tank was revised. New colour combinations made the cabin brighter, and it was also quieter as sound-proofing was uprated. There was still just the multi-function instrument ahead of the driver, providing the speedometer and subsidiary dynamo and oil pressure warning lights as well as an indicator warning light. Towards the end of 1955, cars destined for the United States were the first Beetles to have flashing-light indicators, low in the front wings outboard of the main lights and incorporated in new tail lights (this improvement had been prompted by some State regulations

which meant that dealers had to contrive indicators on the bumpers). Incidentally, twin exhaust pipes were introduced for 1956 (20 years later the U.S.-market fuel-injection Beetle reverted to a single pipe). Plastics material replaced the fabric in the sun-roof, and that lasted until 1964 when a steel sun-roof was introduced.

The 1955 models were the last to be identified by chassis numbers related to calendar years; from that year, Volkswagen's model years ran August-July so that cars coming off the line late in 1955 were 1956 models.

Through the second half of the Fifties, tuning specialists increasingly responded to a predictable enthusiast demand, concentrating on engines but also offering suspension modifications. Uprated engine components and conversions by companies such as Okrasa were popular on both sides of the Atlantic, while Fischer, Judson and Horrocks listed supercharger kits.

The main-line Beetle story was one of continuing evolution, so there are few natural breaks and landmarks tended to be in the form of production achievements. However, the introduction of the large near-rectangular rear window in 1958 signalled the opening of a new chapter for Beetle buffs.

Specifications **Type 1, 1945 onward**		**1200, 1955 onwards**	
Engine:	*4 cylinders, horizontally opposed, air-cooled; 75 x 64 mm, 1131 cc; 25 bhp at 3300 rpm*	**Engine:**	*4 cylinders, horizontally opposed, air-cooled; 77 x 64 mm, 1192 cc; 30 bhp at 3400 rpm*
Transmission:	*Four-speed manual gearbox*	**Transmission:**	*Four-speed manual gearbox*
Suspension:	*Front, independent by torsion bars and trailing arms, hydraulic shock absorbers; rear, independent, swing axle, radius arms and torsion bars, hydraulic shock absorbers*	**Suspension:**	*Front, independent by torsion bars and trailing arms, hydraulic shock absorbers; rear, independent, swing axle, radius arms and torsion bars, hydraulic shock absorbers*
Brakes:	*Drum*	**Brakes:**	*Drum*
Dimensions:	*Wheelbase, 94.5 in (240 cm); front track, 51 in (129.5 cm); rear track, 49 in (124.5 cm); weight, 1590 lb (721 kg)*	**Dimensions:**	*Wheelbase, 94.5 in (240 cm); front track, 51 in (129.5 cm); rear track, 49 in (124.5 cm); weight, 1600 lb (726 kg)*
Maximum speed:	*57 mph (92 km/h)*	**Maximum speed:**	*68 mph (109.4 km/h).*

ABOVE AND ABOVE LEFT
The interior of the oval-window cars was a little less austere than the early models. This well-used but obviously treasured car shows the column-mounted indicator stalk dating from 1952, the cranked gear lever that came in the mid-Fifties, and the conventional accelerator pedal that replaced the awkward roller type in 1958, as well as details such as the parcel shelf. In the nose the spare wheel promises some protection for the fuel tank. The headlight peaks were familiar optional extras.

3. KARMANN-GHIA INTERLUDE

BELOW

The Karmann-Ghia coupé as it was introduced.

INSET

Few changes were made to the engine, but an air filter from the Transporter had to be fitted, in place of the oil bath filter, to reduce the height of the unit. The battery was also located in the engine compartment.

After the cabriolets, Volkswagen was reluctant to agree to more variations on the Beetle theme: in particular, Nordhoff was firmly committed to the one-model policy as far as cars were concerned, and to the goals of ever-increasing production and sales. Porsche could hardly be denied, of course, and from that infant company's 356, in 1949, allegiances were strong. Beyond that, the platform chassis was attractive to specialists, while other Beetle components were used by constructors such as Wolfgang Denzel in the Fifties.

Dr Wilhelm Karmann pressed the case for an association in a sports car, as soon as his company's cabriolet Beetle was in production in 1949, and he persisted. In 1953 he enlisted Luigi Segre of Ghia as an ally, and late that year the prototype of the car that was to link the names of their two companies was completed. It is not clear who styled it. Among prominent candidates were Virgil Exner (whose designs for Chrysler were executed by Ghia) and Mario Boano:

however, it could be that commercial director Segre managed to combine their ideas with the work of others in the studio. It is just possible.

Ghia had to buy a Beetle as a start point and throw away its body. In its place, and on the standard Beetle wheelbase, the Italian coachbuilder mounted a sleek coupé body. This persuaded Nordhoff to bless the project, subject to realistic commercial propositions, for by Volkswagen standards of the Fifties this was to be an expensive car. Volkswagen was to supply rolling chassis to Karmann, and complete cars were to be sold through VW dealers. Moreover, it was to have a Volkswagen type number (the coupé was 143, the later convertible was to be 141).

The production side was by no means straightforward. Karmann had to arrange for wider platform panels to be pressed (the floorpan was 6.3-in/16-cm wider), and strengthening side members had to be added. Under its rounded – almost voluptuous – lines the body was complex,

with numerous internal pressings to be welded together, and to the main panels. The body was completed before it was bolted to the chassis.

Mechanically, the Karmann-Ghia was a Beetle, with tiny changes such as the relocation of the battery in the engine compartment (in the Beetle it was under the rear seat) and in the angle of the steering column. An anti-roll bar was added at the front, and some contemporaries found this had disproportionate roadholding benefits (the lower centre of gravity and the better aerodynamics helped, too). The coupé was launched in 1955 with the 30 bhp engine, later gaining the uprated 34 bhp unit. In the United States, particularly, there were efforts to counter this relative lack of power with supercharged conversions, although the tight engine deck made for installation problems (hence established conversions such as the Fischer kit would not fit).

The cockpit was sporting in some respects, with two fully adjustable seats, plus a meagre rear bench with a folding back to give useful luggage space (there was more room in the nose, too, behind the standard revised 8-gallon/36-litre + 1-gallon/4.5-litre reserve tank). The column was fixed, and the Beetle wheel was retained until 1957 when a Karmann wheel incorporating the VW badge was introduced. The fascia was basic, and the speedometer was paired with a similar-size clock; there was no fuel gauge, but the reserve tap arrangement was carried over from the Beetle. Visibility was good – very good for the Fifties – and built quality was highly rated. Ventilation was not, for the airflow from the nose intakes, which could be blended with heater air, was inadequate, while there were no quarter lights and the rear side

windows were fixed.

Whoever designed it, the body was attractive, and efficient. The Karmann-Ghia coupé was heavier than the saloon, and this exacted a penalty in acceleration (0-50 mph/0-80 km/h taking 18.2 sec). Better aerodynamics paid a dividend when it came to top speed, with 76 mph (122 km/h) possible.

This Karmann-Ghia was no road-burner, and it was not a sports car – among sports cars only the bluff Morgan 4/4 with an engine of similar capacity had a similarly low top speed (but distinctly better acceleration). So the Karmann-Ghia was bought for its looks and reputation for quality – and it sold astonishingly well.

A cabriolet was inevitable, and came in autumn 1957 for the 1958 model year and in left-hand-drive form only as it was correctly assumed that the American market would take most of the early production of this Type 141; a right-hand-drive version (Type 142) was launched for 1960.

Further strengthening was required to compensate for the loss of the roof's contribution to stiffness. The soft-top was exemplary, with a durable outer skin and cloth headlining sandwiching a hair filling, but with the drawback of a plastics rear window until 1969. Erection was straightforward; lowered, it folded into the rear luggage compartment ahead of the engine, and a press-studded hood bag kept it tidy. The cabriolet was a little heavier than the coupé, so there was a slight loss of performance.

As the cabriolet was introduced, the coupé was revised in details, and the two were then run in parallel. From the outset, the cabriolet had a fuel gauge, and as this was also fitted to the coupé, that model lost the reserve tap. The reworked and more powerful engine from the saloon came in 1961 but gave no performance improvements as weights had crept up. The 1300 engine of 1966 lifted the top speeds of both cars by around 2 mph (3 km/h).

For 1967 the Karmann-Ghias were badged '1500' as the 44-bhp 1493-cc engine was introduced, giving the coupé an 82-mph (132-km/h) maximum speed. There was another marginal gain with the 50 bhp 1584 cc '1303S' engine which came for 1971, although not to 90 mph (145 km/h) claimed in publicity.

Meanwhile, front disc brakes were an innovation in 1965 when the track was increased (only fractionally at the front). In 1968 a semi-automatic gearbox was offered, and with it a modified rear suspension. From the summer of 1967 an external fuel filler cap meant that the nose compartment no longer had to be opened to refuel. Also, in common with the Beetle, items such as 12-volt electrics and dual-circuit brakes were introduced. Larger parking lights, stop lights, indicators and hazard-warning lights followed industry trends or legal requirements, as did a collapsible steering column.

There were few changes towards the end of the life of the Type 1 Karmann-Ghia, although in the Seventies cockpit revisions such as the 'safety' four-spoke steering wheel in 1972 made both versions seem more up to date.

A larger companion, the Karmann-Ghia based on the VW 1500 (Type 3), was introduced in 1962, and discontinued in 1969 when just over 42,000 had been built. So just as the 1500 saloon was not a successor to the Beetle (however much it was sometimes regarded as 'a Beetle in disguise'), this coupé in no way lived up to the first Karmann-Ghia coupé and cabriolet.

These were successful by any standards. They should never be assessed as sports cars, and certainly not as high-performance cars – in these respects their looks misled. They were deservedly popular as distinctive touring or cruising cars, well built and reliable, and in their later years well-mannered, too. The last were built in 1974, when production at Osnabrück had reached 363,401 coupés and 80,899 cabriolets.

Large tail lights complement the wrap-round indicators at the nose and show that this is a convertible of the Seventies. The Karmann-Ghia badge behind the front wheel arch was not unusual, but this car also has a VW badge ahead of the rear wheels.

Specifications Type 1, Karmann-Ghia		
Engine:	*4 cylinders; horizontally opposed, air-cooled; 1955-65: 77 x 64 mm, 1192 cc; 30 bhp at 3300 rpm (from 1960, 34 bhp); subsequently 1285 cc, 1493 cc, 1584 cc, as Beetles*	
Transmission:	*Four-speed manual gearbox*	
Suspension:	*Front, independent by torsion bars and trailing arms, shock absorbers, anti-roll bar; rear, independent by swing axle, radius arms and torsion bars, shock absorbers*	
Brakes:	*Drum; front discs from 1965*	
Dimensions:	*Wheelbase, 94.5 in (240 cm); front track, 51 in (129.5 cm); rear track, 49 in (124.5 cm), from 1966 51 in (129.5 cm): weight 1,742 lb (790 kg), rising to 1,918 lb (870 kg) on late cars*	
Maximum speed:	*76 mph (122 km/h), rising to a claimed 90 mph (145 km/h) with 1303S engine in 1973*	

4. BOOM YEARS

ABOVE
Early Sixties Beetles on a used car lot in the following decade, when the appreciation of their value as everyday transport tended to increase (the car in the foreground is a 1964 model).

BELOW RIGHT
A separate fuel gauge was fitted from 1962 until 1966 (this is one of the later cars, with black control knobs).

During the Fifties the layout of the Beetle was questioned, but in general, new popular models followed the Beetle pattern, or the traditional front engine/rear drive format, until the Mini came at the end of the decade. However, no new cars of the Fifties had such distinctive beetle-like lines, or trailed such distinctive sounds. None inspired such owner loyalty or enjoyed such wide cult status, often in the face of suspicions that image might be taking over from the realities of specification and capability.

Clever marketing played its part, especially in publicity in the United States through the Sixties when Volkswagen became a major force in the world's largest single market. By the end of that decade, more than 3 million Beetles – Bugs, if you prefer – had been sold in America. In the mid-Sixties, too, production had started in Mexico, where it was to run on towards the Millenium.

The Beetle for the 1960 model year was the 1200, in standard and de luxe forms. A continuing policy of small incremental improvements had given it slightly revised headlight positions and flashing turn indicators had been positioned atop the wings of U.S.-

bound cars (those for other markets were soon to follow). Engine and gearbox had been tilted forward a little more and the suspension geometry changed to improve handling. The torsion bars were made more progressive, to improve the ride. None of this was fundamental, and while the car was improved, the Beetle was slipping behind its competitors in terms of measured performance. At this time cars were being delivered which did not have the legendary rust-resistant qualities: VW used poor-quality steel for a brief period (naturally, this did not become immediately obvious).

A first move towards catching up came in the summer of 1960 in the form of a substantially reworked engine. Bore and stroke were unchanged, but there were modifications from crankcase and crankshaft to pushrods and carburetter, and the compression ratio was raised to 7:1. This gave a power increase of some 12 per cent which was coupled with a lower (but still high) final-drive ratio to obtain worthwhile gains in acceleration, while the top speed went up to 72 mph (116 km/h).

Beyond that, the redesigned gearbox had synchromesh on all four gears. Its operation was light, and the ratios well chosen; the higher top gear ratio combined with the car's effective aerodynamics to give exceptional steady speed fuel consumption figures.

Suspension modifications reduced the notorious oversteer – it was still there, but not so pronounced – and made the Beetle more trustworthy in cross-winds. The steering was still positive, but no longer quite so light as it had been (an hydraulic steering damper had been

introduced). The brakes were rated good as the Sixties opened, although they were to be criticized later in the decade.

A first cockpit impression was still one of solidity, apart from occasional hints that the body was perhaps not quite as rigid as a unitary-constructed one; this was borne out as much by rough-road travel as by the time-honoured clunk of a closing door (intriguingly, the Porsche Büro had put forward a unitary-construction proposal for the Beetle during the Second World War). The pillars, by this time, were beginning to seem thick and the luggage arrangements less than adequate despite the additional space in the nose compartment, made possible by a revised fuel tank. Effective windscreen demisting still depended on opening a window. Engine cooling air which had been heated as it passed round the power unit still provided the simple heating, controlled by an adjustable valve, but still largely

dependent on engine speed, so that at low road speeds it provided little warmth. The basic 'fresh air' heating system seldom provided air that was fresh, and its output depended on engine speed. Noise from the engine and cooling fan could still be intrusive, although it had been reduced by the end of the Fifties.

Overall, the cockpit was sensibly equipped – not lavishly, even in de luxe cars, but entirely adequately once a fuel gauge was fitted from 1962. Trim had been improved towards the end of the Fifties, and was again in 1963-64 cars; minor controls were modified; there was a dished steering wheel with a horn ring in 1960-65, then a spoke-mounted horn button, until the half-ring reappeared.

If anything, the performance of the 1200 fell off a little in the following years. A road test in *Autocar*, in 1962, recorded a 73-mph (117.5-km/h) top speed, but a car tested by *Motor* in

A 1964 cabriolet in immaculate condition. This 1200 has been sensibly embellished with chrome stoneguards, and it has the type of bumper usually associated with U.S.-market cars.

ABOVE
The 1600 launched for the 1967
model year was significant for its
1493cc engine, suspension revisions
that improved road behaviour
despite the crossply tyres still fitted
by the factory, and its effective disc
brakes (OPPOSITE ABOVE) at the
front. The seats (RIGHT) made the
interior look plusher, and details
such as door locks were revised.

1963 had a mean maximum speed of 70 mph (113 km/h), and a 0-50 mph (0-80 km/h) acceleration time of 18.6 seconds. These figures did not compare well with other cars in the class.

Late in 1961, production reached 5 million, and it exceeded 800,000 in a single year for the first time, in 1962. There were some misgivings about the Beetle's prospects within VW and in wider German economic and industrial circles, and there was the distraction of the troublesome 1500 (Type 3). But there was a major commitment to the Beetle's future, in a plant at Emden dedicated to its manufacture for export, that was to start operations in 1964.

Beetle changes through this period really were in details, and one to be regretted was the disappearance of the attractive Wolfsburg badge from 1963 cars. That year was chosen by Volkswagen to mark its 25th anniversary as a car manufacturer, rather oddly as prototypes of the Beetle had appeared before 1938, and the KdF-Wagen was not in production in 1938.

Output reached a million in a calendar year in 1965 (plus some 60,000 built in Brazil) and the summer brought the 1300 for the 1966 model year. Outwardly distinguished by badging at the rear, this had a 1285-cc engine, combining the existing 77-mm bore with the 69-mm stroke from the Type 3. It was initially rated at 40 bhp at 4000 rpm in DIN terms, or a quoted 50 bhp by the SAE system, which gave a top speed of 76 mph (122 km/h), with 0-50 mph (0-80 km/h) achieved in 15.2 seconds, according to a road test

in *Motor*. This engine was to be continued until 1975 and for its last five years gave 44 bhp at 4100 rpm.

Only a year after the 1300, the Beetle 1500 was announced. This had a 1493-cc engine, with the same dimensions as the Type 2 vehicles, to give 44 bhp DIN at 4000 rpm (or 53 bhp SAE), with improved torque. Incidentally, this version of the boxer engine had already been used in independent Beetle conversions.

Top speed of the European version of the 1500 was 84 mph (135 km/h), while the 0-50 mph (0-80 km/h) acceleration time was cut to 14.5 seconds. A U.S. test by *Road & Track* recorded a 78-mph (125-km/h) maximum speed, with 0-50 mph achieved in 14.8 seconds. The *Motor* testers found this model a fraction slower, but shaved more than a second from that acceleration time: although the Beetle was still geared to ensure mechanical durability, another final drive ratio change, from 4.37:1 to 4.125:1, contributed to its improved acceleration.

There was more to this model change. 'European' 1500 cars had disc brakes at the front although, at announcement, cars destined for North America still had drums all round. All had revised rear suspension, with softer torsion bars, which had the effect of increasing front roll stiffness. An 'anti-bump bar' or 'compensator

A standard late-Sixties Beetle, serving its family transport role.

bar' (in effect, an anti-roll bar) made for progressive stiffening as the rear wheels were deflected upwards. Coupled with a 1.8-in/4.6-cm increase in rear track, this was reckoned to make the onset of the dreaded oversteer more predictable. These changes went some way to meet complaints by the then-vociferous American road safety lobby (who remembers Ralph Nader now?) Improved ride was a bonus.

Headlights were necessarily upright, to meet U.S. requirements, the engine cover grew a modest bulge and there were improvements in fittings, such as the door locks and seat mountings. These changes were carried through to other models in the Beetle range. The 1200 was little publicized by the mid-Sixties when it was continued mainly for the German market as the 1200A; the 1300 was in standard and de luxe forms, while the 1500 was the only version exported to the United States.

Motor rated the 1500 '*much more lively and pleasant to drive ... a great improvement in cornering power and road adhesion ... the best small Volkswagen yet*'. However, it did suggest

that it should not be compared with other 1.5-litre cars, rather with 1.1–1.3-litre models. Here, its only clear advantage was in its touring fuel consumption – a benefit stemming from that lightly-stressed, low-revving engine (on the other hand, its overall fuel consumption for the 1,026-mile/1,651-km test was less impressive at 26 mpg, or 10.9 litres/100 km).

For 1967, VW offered the 1500 with a semi-automatic transmission (only the larger 1600 Volkswagen had a fully automatic option, although the Beetle carried the same emblem on its engine cover). In common with other European manufacturers such as Fiat and NSU, Volkswagen used its conventional gearbox with just three ratios, coupled to a torque converter. The gear lever was retained and the clutch was servo-operated, with a switch at the base of the gear lever. The second, third and top gear ratios were retained (torque multiplication meant that there was no starting handicap in the deletion of first gear), and the final drive ratio was lowered. The operating technique was not demanding, but it was possible to change gear faster with the excellent manual gearbox. That complemented the car's more sporting handling.

The new transmission altered the weight distribution, and to avoid handling regression the rear suspension was revised. This involved abandoning the swing axle and replacing it with jointed drive shafts. Torsion bar springing was retained, with second diagonal locating links added, to give semi-trailing arm suspension. This resulted in a much lower roll centre, and further subdued that oversteer.

The automatic 1500 lost out in top speed (75 mph/121 km/h), but acceleration was slightly better, and it compared well with other small cars with automatic transmission. Fuel consumption suffered, a reliable overall figure being 25.2 mpg (11.2 litres/100 km).

This transmission was available on the 1300 Beetle from 1969, but it never became widely popular. However, the revised suspension became sought after, as drivers of regular Beetles watched Beetles with rear wheels that did not tuck in when cornering. It was available on manual gearbox 1500s sold in the United States in 1969,

and that led to some 're-imports' for German customers.

After that burst of innovation, the Sixties ended with minor enhancements – not that these were unwelcome. For 1968 there was a fresh-air ventilation system in the 1300 and 1500 (to be improved for 1970), outwardly identified by an intake grille ahead of the windscreen; the dual-circuit braking and the 12-volt electrics already standard on U.S.-market 1500s were specified for the 1300 and 1500 in Europe; the fuel filler was under a flap high on the right-hand side of the nose compartment, behind the wing; a fuel gauge was incorporated in the speedometer on the revised fascia; safety modifications included a collapsible steering column and front seat head restraints (which made the rear a little claustrophobic). Outwardly, there were larger bumpers, with no overriders.

In this form the 1300 was continued into the Seventies, together with the 1200 Export. The basic 1200 did not have all the improvements, for example the 12-volt electrics. But 1970 saw a real effort to uprate the Beetle for the new

A 1969 1300L, with the popular Lemmerz wheels marketed by a German accessories company. This view also shows the flap covering the fuel filler, just ahead of the door.

The torsion-bar suspension model was continued in 1200 and 1300 forms after the introduction of the 1302 with MacPherson strut front suspension. This 1970 model year 1300 (ABOVE) is fully representative of the older type, which in Latin American production was to outlive the Super Beetle. This side view emphasizes the basic unchanging shape, while the open nose compartment (RIGHT) once again shows how much space the reclining spare wheel demanded (the overriders below it were optional, incidentally), while the engine compartment (OPPOSITE BELOW) gives an impression that it contains more machinery than earlier models.

The interior (OPPOSITE ABOVE) is in showroom condition, and the fascia has soft black knobs introduced as a minor contribution to safety in the Sixties.

decade, with basic departures from the Thirties design; apart from the three-year old suspension revisions, these were the first fundamental changes.

Despite misgivings, and even short-time working at Wolfsburg in 1967, Beetle sales were still crucial to Volkswagen, particularly in the still-growing American market. Annual production exceeded a million in 1968-1971, and even in 1967 Volkswagen was the fifth-largest automobile manufacturer. Taking all this into consideration, it seemed no more than appropriate that construction work should have started on its large proving ground some 15 miles north of Wolfsburg (this was to be completed in 1972).

Heinrich Nordhoff was preparing to step aside, and in 1968 gave way to one of his assistant directors, Dr Kurt Lotz (a one-time BBC executive in Germany). Plans were accelerated as Nordhoff suffered a fatal heart attack. He had steered the company through two decades and to great prosperity. He left it with a fairly wide product range, well removed from the one-model car policy he had once advocated so strongly. In 1970, this comprised Beetles, the Karmann-Ghia pair, the 1600s in 16 specifications, the 411 in six forms, the Volkswagen-Porsche 914, the 181 four-seat canvas-top utility vehicle and the commercial types. None of the cars promised to become a successor to the Beetle, but the company had taken over NSU and Audi, and therein lay the key to its future. Meanwhile, the Beetle was still king, with an overdue rejuvenation about to come.

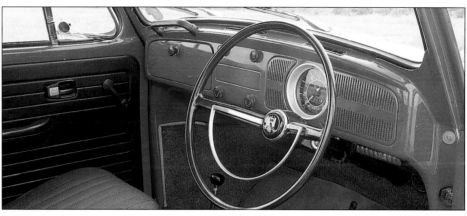

Specifications 1200, from 1960		
Engine:	4 cylinders, horizontally opposed, air-cooled; 77 x 64 mm, 1192 cc; 34 bhp at 3600 rpm	
Transmission:	Four-speed manual gearbox	
Suspension:	Front, independent by torsion bars and	
trailing	arms, hydraulic shock absorbers; rear, independent, swing	
axle,	radius arms and torsion bars, hydraulic shock absorbers	
Brakes:	Drum	
Dimensions:	Wheelbase, 94.5 in (240 cm); front track, 51 in (129.5 cm); rear track, 49 in (124.5 cm); weight, 1,610 lb (730 kg)	
Maximum speed:	72 mph (116 km/h)	

1300		
Engine:	4 cylinders, horizontally opposed, air-cooled; 77 x 69 mm, 1285 cc; 40 bhp at 4000 rpm	
Transmission:	Four-speed manual gearbox	
Suspension:	Front, independent by torsion bars and	
trailing	arms, hydraulic shock absorbers; rear, independent, swing	
axle,	radius arms and torsion bars, hydraulic shock absorbers	

Brakes:	Drum	
Dimensions:	Wheelbase, 94.5 in (240 cm); front track, 51 in (129.5 cm); rear track, 49 in (124.5 cm) until 1966, then 53.5 in (136 cm); weight, 1,675 lb (760 kg)	
Maximum speed:	76 mph (122 km/h)	

1500		
Engine:	4 cylinders, horizontally opposed, air-cooled; 83 x 69 mm, 1493 cc; 44 bhp at 4000 rpm	
Transmission:	Four-speed manual or three-speed semi-automatic gearbox	
Suspension:	Front, independent by torsion bars and trailing arms, hydraulic shock absorbers; rear, independent, swing axle, radius arms and torsion bars, hydraulic shock absorbers (semi-automatic cars: independent, drive shafts and semi-trailing arms, torsion bars, hydraulic shock absorbers)	
Brakes:	Disc front, drum rear	
Dimensions:	Wheelbase, 94.5 in (240 cm); front track, 51 in (129.5 cm); rear track, 53 in (134.5 cm); weight, 1,808 lb (820 kg)	
Maximum speed:	84 mph (135 km/h)	

5. VARIATIONS – MILITARY AND WORKING SPIN-OFFS

ABOVE

A well-loaded Kübelwagen goes to war. This Afrika Korps vehicle has the special tyres adopted for desert conditions. A Kübelwagen captured in this theatre was the first VW to be tested in non-German hands. Unladen, the vehicle sat high on its suspension, and this preserved Type 82 (OPPOSITE) has the headlight arrangement best suited to everyday roads.

No sooner was the KdF-Wagen designed than thoughts turned to possible derivatives, and in the unhealthy nationalistic climate of Germany in the Thirties that meant possible military uses. The layout and the platform chassis, and the promise of sturdy simplicity in many components, were in its favour; against it were some of the schisms that so often divided the German arms industry and forces through the Hitler years.

An adaptation as a light gun-carrier was proposed as early as 1934, and one of the VW30 chassis was converted for this role in 1937. That was not developed, but at the same time the Porsche Büro designed its first Beetle off-road derivative. The prototype of this Type 62 had typically stark military lines, with a canvas top and 'doors', and rode on 19-inch wheels to increase its ground clearance.

It was developed as the Type 82, which was to become familiar as the Kübelwagen, nicknamed for its four bucket seats. This had more purposeful lines, with a steel body pressed by Ambi-Budd, four simple steel doors and

improved weather protection. There was a large fuel tank in the angular nose, with the spare wheel mounted externally above it. The suspension was modified to accommodate final drive changes, and this meant that the ground clearance was increased, which in turn allowed the use of 16-inch wheels.

The Kübelwagen was only a little heavier than the KdF-Wagen, but from 1943 a 25-bhp 1131-cc engine took the place of the 22.5-bhp 985-cc unit. This was actually called for by the considerably heavier Schwimmwagen offshoot, rather than to cope with military overloading. Both engines were to be widely used as portable power units, and the larger version was to be adopted for the post-war Beetle.

By all accounts, the Kübelwagen was popular with the German army, from rankers to generals, for its all-round utility and its ability to plough through mud, snow or sand. Yet production, at just over 50,000, was modest, partly because of bureaucracy and bungling in the army's procurement departments.

Many variants were to appear. A four-wheel-drive version (Porsche Types 86 and 87) did not progress beyond the prototype stages but led to the famous Schwimmwagen amphibious vehicle. This first appeared as the Type 128 in 1940 and reached its definitive form as the Type 166 in 1942 (it needed the 25 bhp engine to meet the military requirement for an 80-km/h/50-mph road speed and a 10-km/h/6.2-mph water speed).

It had a doorless four-seat body, and details such as waterproofed electrics to guard against moisture in the hull. Four-wheel-drive was standard, and there was a dog clutch to take power to the three-blade propeller, which was manually lowered and retracted.

The Schwimmwagen was successful, with versatility extending beyond swimming, for example to off-road climbing ability. But it was also costly, and by KdF-Wagen standards complex, so production was limited to around 15,000 in 1942-44 – figures between 14,000 and 16,000 have been quoted.

In 1943 the Kübelwagen chassis and specialized transmission was married to the KdF-Wagen body to create the Kommandeurwagen. This had a canvas roof, and appeared in three-

and four-seat forms; several hundred were built, 1942-44.

Porsche's engine studies during the Second World War included a wood-gas unit for the Beetle, rated at 12 bhp, a sleeve-valve unit, supercharged and turbocharged versions of the flat four in efforts to produce the power required for some military purposes, a fuel-injection flat four, and a diesel version (VW returned to this possibility in 1951 but abandoned it as there was too little power and too much noise).

The Type 92 Kommandeurwagen links into the 1945 revival, simply because parts were available as hand-to-mouth VW production started. At the same time, some vans and pick-up trucks were built, based on the Kübelwagen and following a wartime project.

Another echo of the Kübelwagen came in open conversions of Beetle saloons, mainly for police use. Before it introduced its shapely cabriolet, Hebmüller built some which normally had canvas 'doors'; a few were built by Papler, with proper doors, and in Austria Tatra built a batch on similar lines for police and army use in 1950-51.

The Kübelwagen with snow tracks was designated Type 155.

By that time the Volkswagen Type 2, the Transporter, was in production. It is within the scope of this book as it owed its origins to Beetle components and British ingenuity, and it was destined to be produced by the million (the millionth was completed in 1962). A British manager conceived a flat-bed factory runabout using available parts; Dutch VW importer Ben Pon saw this as the basis of a van/pick-up, and promoted the idea; the project was taking shape as Nordhoff was appointed, and under his régime it surged ahead.

The Beetle 1131 cc engine and running gear in beefed-up form was used, with a more substantial chassis. It came in 1950 as the Kombi, as a van that could be fitted with seats – an early MPV, in fact – and the Microbus that was announced within months.

This Type 2 was offered in several forms and motor caravan (or camper) conversions were to become familiar, the first appearing in 1951. Through the following years it was continually uprated, for example, with the 1192 cc engine from 1954, and production was moved to a purpose-built factory in 1956. Fundamental change came when a diesel option was offered in

1969, and ten years later an entirely new type took its place.

The coachbuilder responsible for the first Type 2 motor-caravan conversion, Westfalia-Werk, also built the bodies for the Type 147 van on the Beetle chassis and running gear. Some 7,500 were produced, including batches for the German and Swiss Post Offices.

Volkswagen (Australia) used some Beetle components in its Country Buggy, introduced in 1968. This simple and angular vehicle had a short production life in Australia, but some were later built in Indonesia. To a degree, it ran in parallel with Germany's Type 181, and it was tested and approved by Wolfsburg. Incidentally, the DMG Sakbayan, built in the Philippines at the end of the Seventies, had even plainer lines, its body comprising flat panels and windows. This five-seat, three-door utility was powered by the 1493 cc engine in 38-bhp form.

Type 181 recalled the Kübelwagen, in its layout, its lines and its higher ground clearance. Intended as a no-nonsense working vehicle, it used the floorpan in modified Type 1 Karmann-Ghia form, with angular bodywork. The 1.5 litre 44-bhp engine gave the first 181s a claimed road

TOP
A British officer appears relieved that a 1945 Schwimmwagen demonstration voyage on the Mittelland canal, near the Wolfsburg factory, is over (the existence of this waterway was one factor in locating the KdF plant). The Schwimmwagen had a doorless body and this one (LEFT) is already prepared for its waterborne role, with propeller lowered.

ABOVE

*This painstakingly restored 1943
Type 82 comprises a KdF-Wagen
saloon body on a Kübelwagen
chassis, and thus represents Second
World War vehicles and some of the
first production Volkswagens, which
'used up' spare military chassis
after the war. Even the sickle
bumper overriders are appropriate
to the late Forties. The engine,
(ABOVE RIGHT) compares with
later cars – all relate instantly.*

RIGHT

*Hebmüller built a small number of
very open conversions for police use
in the late Forties, most with canvas
'doors' but a few with four metal
doors. These were apparently
intended for parade or city patrol
use, not as chase cars! A few similar
conversions were also built by other
companies.*

speed of 66 mph (107 km/h). However, that was not the main point, for this was laid down for military use (and it was sold to armies), then found wider utility uses, and was to be adopted as a recreational vehicle, particularly in climates where reliable weather protection was not a first requirement. To a degree, its looks deceived, for it did not have the four-wheel-drive that would have made it an all-round off-roader.

From the outset, in 1969, it was a successful addition to the VW range. For civilian use, it was marketed as the Safari, and in the United States became well known as 'The Thing'. In 1973 production was transferred from VW's Hanover plant to Mexico. Along the way it gained the revised suspension of the Beetle saloons, and in the Eighties the Puebla-built Safari had the 1.6-litre engine, rated at 48 bhp in 1981, to give a 71-mph (115-km/h) capability.

It was still spartan, with two bucket seats at the front and a rear bench seat that nominally accommodated three. Like the Beetle, it echoed a much earlier period in VW history, reflecting a quality of timelessness.

LEFT
The best known Beetle spin-off was the Type 2, as the Transporter, or in this Microbus form.

BELOW INSET
Type 181 recalled the Kübelwagen, and was introduced as a commercial vehicle. In its recreational form it became known as 'The Thing'. Here it is in fire service colours, in 1977.

6. SUPER BEETLE

While Volkswagen pursued its search for a successor to the Beetle, the life of this classic car was again extended. In some respects time really had caught up with it – nothing could be done about an interior that was narrow and minimal – but capital and development resources had to be devoted to it, and the strength of user allegiances meant that it kept selling.

So 1970 saw the announcement of the 1302 series, the 'Super Beetle', or 'Super Bug', the nickname that was used in North America. The intention had been to designate this new version 1301, but that numerical combination was already being used by another manufacturer.

The 1302 marked a much bigger move away from the Thirties design than the revised rear suspension of the 1968 semi-automatic model. That arrangement was adopted for all 1302 models, while at the front a MacPherson strut layout replaced the transverse torsion bar suspension. This gave better handling and adhesion, and a tighter turning circle.

It also freed space in the nose so that the spare wheel could be laid flat. The design team took the opportunity to reshape the fuel tank and increase its capacity to 9.1 gallons (41.4 litres). The upper surface of the nose was given a distinctive bulge. These changes meant that a lot more luggage could be stowed in the front of the car. To accommodate the suspension changes, the front of the floorpan was modified, giving a 0.8-in (2-cm) wheelbase stretch, while 3.2 in (8 cm) was added to the overall length.

The engine was based on the 1584 cc unit introduced for 1970 model-year American-market cars, to maintain power output and performance there as anti-pollution regulations bit. It was

OPPOSITE

The longer bulging nose distinguished the Super Beetle for the Seventies. The space freed in the nose by the MacPherson suspension and relocated spare wheel (LEFT) meant that front luggage space became really useful.

strengthened with a revised crankcase, the twin-inlet port heads used on the Type 3 1600 engine (already popular with independent Beetle tuning specialists), and other modifications. Its output, 50 bhp DIN or 60 bhp in SAE terms, was slightly less than the 1600, and by no means generous for a 1.6 litre unit in the Seventies though nevertheless a worthwhile improvement on the previous 1500 Beetle engine.

It made the Beetle an 80-mph (say, 130-km/h) car – just – with more flexible top-gear performance that was useful for cruising, and there was a side advantage as some of the air-cooled flat-four noises were subdued. There was a penalty to be paid in fuel consumption, and as the slightly larger fuel tank did not wholly compensate, the car's range was reduced.

Directional stability was questioned again, for the relatively high body and the 44/56 weight distribution meant that the car could still react badly to side-winds. Generally, the ride was not improved to the same degree as handling, some testers finding insufficient travel in the suspension, to the extent that it could bottom out over quite gentle road undulations, while others rated it bouncier than with the old torsion bar set-up. The disc/drum combination on 'European-specification' cars made for sure braking, but cars destined for the United States still had drum brakes all round, and these called for well-developed leg muscles in an emergency stop.

Some effort was put into cabin improvements, the most valuable being the introduction of extractor vents for the through-flow ventilation, although these little half-moon shapes behind the rear side windows were not large enough to be fully effective. There was still a single round dial facing the driver, seen through the upper quadrant of the two-spoke steering wheel. Its main function was still as a speedometer, and it also incorporated a fuel gauge, ignition light, indicator and main-beam tell-tales, oil pressure light and total distance recorder. As ever, it was set in a painted metal fascia, for a padded version was offered in only a few markets. However, there was a padded steering wheel from 1971.

The seats were still firm and in the Seventies seemed small and too flat to be supportive. Visibility was not good, for the pillars now seemed thick and to the rear the base of the window was high. Its depth was increased a little for 1971 when the engine cover louvres below it were altered (and the water drainage tray beneath it was discontinued, which was not an improvement in wet weather!)

In terms of measured performance, *Motor* recorded a mean top speed of 79.7 mph (128 km/h) in its road test, while *Autocar* and *Road & Track* found this model fractionally slower. Acceleration to 50 mph (80 km/h) from rest took 12.6 seconds in the *Motor* test, while *Autocar* testers managed it in 12.2 seconds and *Road & Track* recorded an even faster time of 12.0 seconds. Overall fuel consumption in the *Motor* test was 23 mpg (12.3 litres/100 km). Those figures were achieved with the 1302S, the 1.6 litre model. There was also a 1320L, with a 1.3 litre engine which had the new cylinder heads, but still had drum brakes at the front.

Meanwhile, the 'old' 1200 with the boxer engine rated at 34 bhp and the 1300 were continued, and so was the 1970 1.6 litre type, to give VW dealers a price leader in the United States. For 1972 the 1200 at last got 12-volt electrics, so another link with the original Volkswagen was broken. The year it was announced, 1971, was the last time Beetle production in Germany exceeded a million units (overall, production in other countries kept it

above a million for another two years).

The padded wheel already mentioned was a response to American safety requirements which found a ready echo in German safety awareness, and the fascia was revamped. Of greater interest, a plug-in diagnostic system was introduced, enabling VW dealers to plug into the wiring looms (of all models) to monitor electrical functions. There were also larger disc brakes on the 1302S.

The semi-automatic model was not listed for 1972, and for the next model year there were the last major Beetle changes, in the 1303. Mechanically, this was the same as the 1302, but it looked really different. This was largely due to the rounded 'panoramic' windscreen, and the consequently shortened cover over the nose compartment. The rear wings were wider, too, but not to accommodate fatter tyres, just the large circular lights which it was anticipated would meet any possible forthcoming legal requirements. However, Beetles built in South Africa combined the old wings and the new rear light clusters.

Inside, there was a substantially revised fascia, padded and matt black, with the circular instrument raised and hooded so that its upper part was hidden by the top of the steering wheel, if the driver was tall. The wheel was the four-spoke padded device introduced a little earlier. Rocker switches took the place of rotary switches and the whole ensemble seemed appropriate to a car of the Seventies. But the new seats did not quite match up in this respect.

There were two 1.3-litre models (1303 and 1303S), and two 1.6-litre models (1303LS and 1303LS cabriolet), and soon the first special editions appeared to capture a few more sales. There was, for example, the Jeans Beetle with blue denim seats and 'sports trim' in 1973-74. South Africa also built a 'Fun Bug' and a 'Lux Bug'. There was a 1.6-litre 'GT Beetle', identified by chrome letters on its engine cover, with sports wheels and cloth seat trim (more show than go, was the verdict). The 'Sun Beetle' in 1975 had a sun-roof and sports wheels. The 'Super Bug' name was applied to the 1302S in the United States in 1973-75, and 'La Grande Bug' in 1976-77 combined the 1.6-litre engine with drum brakes and torsion bars all round.

The 'Sports Bug', in the United States, was described by one cynic as 'a customized Super Beetle'. It had $5\frac{1}{2}$J wheels instead of the normal $4\frac{1}{2}$Js, and inside the bucket seats were appropriate to a car with more real performance. It could just exceed 80 mph. That was a little slower than the 1303S tested by *Motor*, which lapped a banked circuit at 82.4 mph (133 km/h).

Meanwhile, the Brazilian plant just continued turning out the flat-windscreen models, with 1.3- and 1.5-litre engines.

In 1973, Volkswagen conclusively took the production record from Ford's Model T. It had first broken this in February 1972 when the 15,007,034th Beetle was completed at Wolfsburg; Ford subsequently 'found' additional Ts, but that 16,561,850 total was surpassed by the Beetle in 1973. The British VW company anticipated that with a Marathon special edition.

However, that notable achievement coincided with a downturn in world trade and a stutter in Germany's economic health. Volkswagen was forced to cut prices to clear stocks in 1972-73, and the mid-Seventies saw it declare large trading losses. The Beetle range was rationalized, and production was concentrated at the Emden plant; the last Wolfsburg Beetle rolled off the line on 1 July 1974, as VW's long-term staple product and the reason for the company's existence at last

made way for a successor, the front-wheel-drive, water-cooled, Golf.

The Beetle was still going strong outside Europe. Brazilian production had started in 1959 following six years assembling CKD (i.e. manufacturer's kits) Beetles. It exceeded the million mark as the Seventies opened, and the second million was completed in half the time. VW do Brasil abandoned the Beetle in favour of a VW- and Ford-based range in the mid-Eighties but, remarkably, 1300 Beetle production was

restarted in August 1993. Earlier, its Beetle variants had included the sporting twin-carburetter Fusca and one with 'alcool' on its engine cover, proclaiming that its engine had been modified to run on sugar-cane-based fuel as the country attempted to escape reliance on imported fuels. Beetle components were used in several local models, such as the Puma, while Brazil had also supplied CKD kits to assembly plants in other countries (including a taxi with a single front seat to facilitate passenger entry, built in Nigeria).

At a more modest level, a quarter of a million Beetles had been built in South Africa, 1951-75, but the last Beetle built in that country was delivered in 1979. There had once been Beetle assembly subsidiaries in some 20 countries around the world, and when German production ended the Beetle was still assembled in Nigeria, Peru, the Philippines, Uruguay and Venezuela, with parts supplied from Brazil. The Mexican subsidiary company was building up a long unbroken record of Beetle production towards the end of the 20th century.

Meanwhile, the Beetle built in Germany was

still refined in details in the second half of the Seventies, such as the energy-absorbing bumpers required for the United States and the front turn indicators repositioned from the tops of the wings to vulnerable positions inset in the bumpers. A Bosch fuel-injected engine was introduced for the U.S. market, in an effort to meet emissions regulations without sacrificing tractable qualities. The 1.3-litre models were dropped from 1976, when everything derived from the 1200, with variants such as the 'luxury' 1200L and the 1200S with a 1.6 litre engine (there seemed to be a contradiction there!)

On 19 January 1978, the last German-built Beetle saloon was completed at Emden, and the company kept it for the VW museum. The final batch was named 'Last Edition', and some 300 of them had silver metallic body paint.

Cabriolet production continued at Karmann's Osnabrück factory for another two years, almost entirely for the American market, where convertibles were rare towards the end of the Seventies. Some of the detail changes were carried over from the saloons, though not all, as the turn indicators remained atop the front wings.

The fuel-injected engine gave a maximum speed of 83 mph (134 km/h), but there were still drum brakes all round. Above all, the cabriolet was still a Beetle, with all the quirks and strengths that implied. It had equally strong appeal for car owners who valued continuity as well as the surf-boarding youth of the West Coast.

Sales had revived after the slump of the mid-Seventies except in Europe, where they remained modest (small numbers were built with the 1.6-litre carburetter engine through to late 1979, and the 1200 engine was optional). It was increasingly expensive to build, and this was reflected in its price, so Karmann built the last cabriolet in January 1980, and kept it for the company museum.

That was not the end of the new Beetle trade in Europe, for there was still a strong demand, especially in Germany. This was met through imports from Volkswagen de Mexico, shipped in for final preparation at Emden and 'officially' supplied to Austria, Holland and Italy as well as Germany.

When the Mexican company had been set up at Puebla in 1964, it was intended that it should

develop a high degree of independence, and this policy paid dividends in the Eighties, a notable milestone being reached early in that decade when it produced the 20-millionth Beetle, in May 1981. It is hardly surprising that it became the largest automobile manufacturer in Mexico, and when the Golf and Jetta were added to its range it once took 72 per cent of the local market. But could anybody have foreseen in 1964 that it would be building Beetles thirty and more years later?

The Mexican Beetles were almost throwbacks with the torsion bar suspension front and rear, and the swing axle, and all the susceptibility to side winds: the 1192 cc engine was rated at 34 bhp, there were drum brakes all round, there was a flat windscreen and modest space in the nose. It has been suggested that this return to Beetle basics appealed to many German customers, and certainly Volkswagen was surprised by sales. These held up well into the Eighties and the last shipment of 3,150 Beetles was processed through Emden in the summer of 1985. Independent attempts to formally import cars into European countries after that foundered

OPPOSITE
A MacPherson strut suspension Cabriolet of the early Seventies. The 1303 production line in 1973 (ABOVE) shows that this was a mainstream operation. The bodyshell in the foreground also shows construction details, including the spare wheel well.

on cost grounds, and sometimes regulations, and
frankly because the Beetle was no longer a
competitive product (it was still possible for
individuals, or their agents, to order one from
Puebla for delivery anywhere in the world).

Changes through the Eighties were
negligible, and apart from the engine were
limited to trim. Died-in-the-wool enthusiasts
could not bring themselves to regard these cars as
run-ons from the German Beetle, and it is
inevitable that build quality and materials were
sometimes questioned. But as specified body
weights increased, the most common allegation
concerning the gauge of body material should not
have been made.

As the Eighties opened, the Mexicans
claimed a top speed of 71 mph (115 km/h) for the
1200L. In 1983 a 1600 was introduced, its 46-
bhp engine giving a claimed 79 mph (127 km/h);
this dropped slightly in the Nineties, to 77 mph
(124 km/h) in 1992. The suspension and brakes,

chassis and body lines were unchanged in this
very tangible echo of the late Forties, if not the
previous decade. It would all have been so
familiar to Dr Porsche. It is quite extraordinary
that so little of his concept had to be changed,
and that in vastly different social and motoring
conditions the Beetle just went on and on and
was still produced as a people's car 60 years after
the first prototype was built in his garage.

**Specifications
1302s**

Engine: *4 cylinders, horizontally opposed, air-cooled; 85 x 69 mm, 1584 cc; 50 bhp at 4000 rpm*

Transmission: *Four-speed manual gearbox*

Suspension: *Front, independent by MacPherson struts with coil springs, transverse link and anti-roll bar; rear, independent, by semi-trailing links, drive shafts, transverse torsion bars*

Brakes: *Disc front/drum rear (some markets, drums all round)*

Dimensions: *Wheelbase, 96 in (244 cm); front track, 53.5 in (136 cm); rear track, 53 in (135 cm); weight, 1,820 lb (825 kg)*

Maximum speed: *80 mph (129 km/h)*

1303S as 1302S, except:

Dimensions: *Weight, 1,900 lb (862 kg)*

Maximum speed: *82 mph (132 km/h)*

1200L (Mexico, 1980) as 1960 1200 (qv), except:

Engine: *Max. power, 34 bhp at 3800 rpm*

Dimensions: *Front track, 51.6 in (131 cm); rear track, 53 in (135 cm); weight, 1,720 lb (780 kg)*

Maximum speed: *71 mph (115 km/h)*

1600 (Mexico, 1992) as 1302S, except:

Engine: *Max. power, 46 bhp at 4000 rpm*

Dimensions: *Wheelbase, 94.5 in (240 cm); front track, 51.6 in (131 cm)*

Brakes: *Drum*

Maximum speed: *77 mph (124 km/h)*

7. SPORTING BEETLE

ABOVE

Outright speed was never regarded as a prime Beetle asset, so it was surprising that the smooth body of this car, built by Hanover VW distributor Petermax Müller, clothed Beetle mechanical elements. It is at the Montlhéry track near Paris for a duration record attempt in 1950.

OPPOSITE

Gar O'Brien attacks the scenery during a Cork 20 Rally – the Beetle was a favourite car in the heyday of Irish rallying in the Fifties and Sixties.

A first reaction to the idea that the Beetle could successfully compete in international motor sport might be one of incredulity. That would be almost understandable, but so very wrong.

The marque might have started to build up motor sport associations as the KdF-Wagen was about to enter production. Porsche was responsible for the Type 64 derivative, a highly-streamlined coupé on the normal chassis, with a twin-carburetter engine giving up to 50 bhp, laid down for the projected Berlin-Rome-Berlin road race, which promised publicity for the autobahn and autostrada systems as well as successful vehicles, and for the Axis alliance. The race was scheduled for Autumn 1939.

The Type 64 had a claimed top speed of 145 km/h (91 mph). Of three built, one was used as a personal car by Ferdinand Porsche during the

Second World War, and another was retrieved to be run in local Austrian events in the late Forties. This car survives.

A more natural contemporary arena would have been the rough-road and long-distance trials encouraged in Germany in the Thirties, where the combination of large wheels and generous ground clearance, weight distribution and sturdy construction, would have made the Beetle a useful contender. Those qualities were to serve it well in post-war rallies, trials and driving tests, and later in rallycross and desert racing.

For many years, Volkswagen steadfastly turned away from motor sport, refusing to consider works teams or development programmes, so preparation was left to entrants, at best local or national concessionaires.

There was an early entry at international level in 1949, when a Beetle finished 43rd (sixth in class behind five British cars) out of 230 entries in the first post-war Monte Carlo Rally. That was a fairly leisurely event, with the result largely decided in special tests, but 43rd in a finishers' list of 166 cars was no mean achievement.

The 27th place in 1950 was even better, and Beetles were placed second in their class in 1952-53, 1956 and 1958. Overall positions in those years varied, but the fifth place achieved by Levy and Kotott in 1956 stands out, being run in generally mild weather conditions that favoured the powerful cars among the 351 starters, such as the winning Jaguar Mk VIIM.

Elsewhere in main-line European events, there had been a class win in the 1951 Tulip Rally for Koks/de Jong/Wisker – a first significant success for the Beetle. In 1953 Koks was second in class. Later in the decade, in 1956-58, there were to be class wins in the Scandinavian classics of the day, the Midnight Sun and Viking Rallies; Jansson and Mors were second overall in the 1958 Midnight Sun, while

Bengtsson and Richard were third overall in that year's Viking.

But the greatest triumphs came in Australia and Africa – the markets Nordhoff looked towards for Beetle sales expansion. In the Fifties the Round Australia Trial under its various sponsor names was a tough rally over long distances, generally more than 10,000 miles/16,000 km and, with the possible exception of the Liège-Rome-Liège, far more demanding than events in Europe. Whitehead and Foreman scored VW's first outright Round Australia victory in 1955, with the Perkins' Beetle second. Sponsorship clashes meant that there were two events in 1956; VW won the team prize, and a Beetle was second overall in the Ampol Trial; Beetles were first, third and fourth in the Mobilgas Trial. In 1957, VWs were 1-2 in the Ampol, and took the first six places in the Mobilgas Trial. The Mobilgas Rally of 1958 was the last in the long, rough and tough tradition, and VWs finished first, second, fourth and fifth.

The Coronation Safari, forerunner of the

Safari, was first run in 1953, and it was won by Dix and Larsen with a Beetle, which was followed home by another VW. There is a retrospective tendency to regard this as VW's first major rally win, but the 1953 event did not really have that status. It soon did, however, and it was to fall to Beetles three more times, in 1954, in 1957 – when there was a VW 1-2-3, headed by the car crewed by Hofmann and Burton – and in 1962. A second place in 1955, class wins through a decade, and the team prize in 1953-55 and 1957-58 backed the Beetle record of victories.

In 1959, the Mediterranean to the Cape Rally was a demanding 8,700-mile (14,000-km) ancestor of more recent marathons or raids and again a Beetle was prominent, one finishing fourth just behind a Land Rover.

Meanwhile, in the Fifties, the Great American Mountain Rally was an attempt to establish international rallying in North America. It hardly succeeded, but rates a footnote in history, as does the fourth place taken by Young and Fendler with a Beetle in 1956. Then there was the second place scored by Stanley and Chelminski in the 1958 Canadian Winter Rally,

with a Karmann-Ghia coupé, a car rarely seen in competition.

The Beetle was highly successful in second-level and national events in Europe, and seemed extraordinarily popular in Ireland – first to sixth places in the 1959 Circuit of Ireland rally bears this out. Competitions in Ireland – trials as well as rallies – also led to an early crop of Beetle-based 'specials', some of which almost anticipated the buggies of the next decade.

More and more, in the Sixties, the Beetle seemed relegated to national and local events, especially the popular British road rallies where the competition element did not depend on the best times over special stages, but where the navigator, with his timing equipment and his ordnance survey maps, came into his own.

Car preparation was minimal by modern standards. Under-car skid plates were generally used ('roo bars in Australia) and a roof-mounted spotlight often identified a rally car. Internally there may have been strengthened seats, but no roll cage. Instruments more informative than the single dial of the production model were normal, and so was the all-important Halda Speedpilot

OPPOSITE
The two Porsche-Austria Beetles are first and fourth in this rallycross quartet at Lydden Hill in 1974, the year they won the European Championship.

ABOVE
This Sand Rail flies the flag that became customary among dune navigators, to warn others of its approach. Once again, the exhaust is typical of a car with the VW flat four.

facing the navigator.

There was some engine and running gear development in Europe, notably by Okrasa. This Frankfurt company was early in the field, with an hydraulic brakes conversion for Beetles in the late Forties, followed by extensive engine tuning and components development work. However, the main impetus was to come from the United States, spurred on by widespread Bug enthusiasm, with tuning specialists such as EMPI.

There was a last word in international rallying. In 1973 Porsche-Austria took the 1302S/1303S and put a concentrated effort into the flat-four 1.6 engine, with a dry-sump conversion, using twin Weber carburetters, special manifolds and heads, twin oil pumps, a compression ratio as high as 9:1, and so on. As much as 126 bhp was wrung from the engine, to be transmitted through a five-speed gearbox. One of its cars was driven to an outright win in the Elba Rally, by Warmbold and Haggbom. In the first season of the World Rally Championship as we now know it, 1973, there were four placings in the top six, notably as future champion Bjorn Waldegaard was sixth in the Swedish Rally. A Beetle last featured among major rally leaders when one was placed eighth in the 1976 Acropolis Rally in Greece.

Beetles were prominent as autocross grew in popularity through the Fifties, although this short-circuit racing on grass never expanded beyond regional levels – happily, for a low-cost 'fun' sport. The peculiarly British activity of trials naturally attracted Beetle owners: the car's traction qualities seemed tailor-made for some of the testing hills in events such as the Exeter Trial and the slippery slopes of production car trials (Mike Hinde won three consecutive championships with Beetles, 1961-63). And Beetles showed surprising agility in the specialized sport of slalom racing and driving tests, or autotests, which once attracted TV coverage.

Rallycross owed its existence to the small screen, for teams were gathered for the 1967 RAC Rally and BBC TV was ready to screen the action when the event was cancelled; a pseudo-special stage was arranged for the television people – as it had been in 1963 – and others saw in this a new branch of motor sport. It caught on locally, expanded into Europe in the Seventies, with an international championship arriving in 1973. In their early years, Beetles were popular cars, in forms from near-original to highly modified.

This Baja Bug in the tough Baja race has several secondary lights.

Franz Wurz took the 1974 European Championship in a Porsche-Austria car, one of its ex-rally Beetles with an engine from the Volkswagen 411 (Type 4), enlarged from 1.8 to 2.4 litres to give up to 180 bhp. Three other Beetle drivers finished in the top ten of the championship table.

That was the last year that Porsche-Austria ran a team, but the cars it had developed were still used, effectively, as two were fourth and fifth in the 1975 European Championship. Above them, in first and second places were Beetles run by the Dutch Conti Adr team, driven by Ces Teurlings and Dick Riefl. Just one Ford Escort, in third place, ruined a Beetle clean sweep of the top six places (Hugh Wheldon was sixth, incidentally).

The Conti Adr cars were even further from the original, for they had Kremer-developed Porsche 3-litre engines, with Porsche gearboxes and limited-slip differentials. That combination was not novel, and one of the more startling machines that might have worried drivers of supposedly high-performance cars in central Germany at the time was a road machine with a Beetle 1303 body concealing VW-Porsche 914

running gear, with a Porsche 2.7-litre 210-bhp straight six mounted ahead of the rear axle. It was created by a Norstadt dealer, and reached 133 mph (213 km/h) on an autobahn.

Tighter regulations meant fewer Beetles in top rallycross until the mid-Eighties when Beetle bodies clothed spectacular mechanical elements, such as four-wheel-drive and turbocharged engines. These machines were really remote from the Beetle origins and appearance, but the 'real thing' remained popular at more modest levels.

Autocross and rallycross pale into insignificance beside desert racing. This had its apex in the Baja 1000, down the long peninsula of Baja California, but it spread through the south-western States and found an echo in the long-distance raids such as the Paris-Dakar. The Beetle's role in its birth and development can hardly be over-estimated, for most of the early dune buggies used Beetle engines, transmission and other components. There were classes for near-standard cars where the Beetle's qualities paid dividends, and the familiar body lines, cut about and high-mounted, maybe, appeared in other types such as 'Baja Bugs' as much as they did on dragsters.

ABOVE
The Bug racer was a close relative,
but the wheels on this Newman-
Dreager Special suggest sprint or
drag car influences.

LEFT
The single seaters encouraged by
desert racing often used Beetle
components. This Sidewinder team
car in the 1974 Baja race was an
example. It is difficult to judge who
is the more stressed by this violent
treatment – the human or the
mechanical frame.

However, the unlimited class soon produced the outright winners, and the Beetle content in these specialized vehicles dwindled through the Seventies, taking their coverage beyond the scope of this book.

The dune buggy has also been a recreational vehicle for more than three decades, and the Beetle was far and away the most important source of components for these exciting little vehicles, used simply for fun (*see* Chapter 8).

Still on the sporting side, Beetles have been raced on circuits, seriously only where stock classes were defined by price, and enjoying some success in Australia where these price categories were once favoured. That apart, they have usually been seen in VW club events, or in the handicap events for near-standard production saloons that were once part of the club racing scene. And there was the Grand Prix of Volkswagens in Nassau, once won by A.J. Foyt.

Formula Vee brought the Volkswagen company into motor sport in the second half of the Sixties. This had its origins in America at the beginning of the decade, when Florida VW dealer Hubert Brundage had a pair of single-seat racing cars built by Nardi, in Italy, around standard Beetle components such as engine and transmission, suspension, brakes and steering. In 1963 Formula Vee racing was sanctioned by the Sports Car Club of America, and in the following year a handful of Vees was demonstrated in Germany. The class caught on in America and spread in Europe, especially in Germany, Austria and Holland (there were some variations, such as the 1200-cc engine stipulated in the United States, and 1300-cc units in Europe and some other countries); the first race in Britain was run in 1967. Apal in Belgium was an early European constructor, but two Austrian builders (Austro Vee and Kaimann) soon became dominant.

This was an entry-level category, and essentially it was intended to give low-cost racing. Its success can be judged by the mid-Eighties estimate that some 7,800 Formula Vee cars had been built. By then, Vee racing had been in decline for several years, for whatever the merits of simplicity and availability it was usually an end in itself (cars for categories such as Formula Ford, and Super Vee, related more closely to more advanced formulae, thus having greater 'training' value). It remained popular in some countries – notably Germany and the United States – and continued at club level in others, such as Britain, in the Nineties.

Utilitarian people's cars and drag racing are at opposite ends of the motoring spectrum, but there is common ground. The hot-rod movement had got under way just before the KdF-Wagen

had got under way just before the KdF-Wagen came into existence, and the first drag strips were operating as the Volkswagen became a serious production car. When its sales took off in the United States, speed components developed by European companies such as Okrasa were available, and their example was soon followed: entrants read the National Hot-Rod Association rules carefully and realized that in some classes the Beetle's weight distribution and traction advantages could be exploited in the home territory of muscle-bound V8 cars.

So in the Sixties Beetles appeared on strips, the first to attract serious attention being the EMPI car developed by owner Joe Vittone and Dean Lowry (this had started life as a 1956 saloon, and was used by Dan Gurney before he became a leading Grand Prix driver). For several years EMPI was the leading name on the strips, and with rebuild following rebuild, its first car became a legendary Bug (as 'Inch Pincher').

Development for this branch of motor sport was rapid, first and foremost in the power units. Engines were enlarged, bored and stroked to more than 2 litres, then special units were built with little or no VW content, but at least with a flat-four layout. Exotic fuels were used, and inevitably turbochargers came. Some 600 bhp was claimed for a 'Beetle' 2.8-litre air-cooled

flat-four in the late Eighties, a unit that had fuel injection for the potent alcohol-based brew and a turbocharger, and a similar output was to be claimed for a 2.4-litre turbo unit in the mid-Nineties.

Transmission systems to cope with power of this order were far removed from the Beetle original, and tubular chassis were also needed to give adequate rigidity. The body might have Beetle lines, perhaps with a rear aerofoil or distorted with a roof chop within permitted dimensions. The overall body aerodynamics were effective enough for a normal road Beetle, but in terms of downforce were poor, while under-car airflow could generate lift at high speeds: the light cars developed in the Eighties could flip, and their drivers could be caught out by cross-winds, so one Beetle quality survived half a century!

Drag racing classes have been numerous, from those for street-legal cars up to the top turbo types, and have been changed frequently. The leading quasi-Beetle turbo cars are capable of terminal speeds around 150 mph, while the close-to-normal cars could be run in bracket, or handicap, racing and give their owners a great deal of fun.

First time in Europe – Gerhard Mitter, a leading German driver of the Sixties and European hill-climb champion, demonstrates an F Vee car at the Eberbach climb.

8. INFINITE VARIETY – FROM SPORTS CARS TO REPLICARS

The Beetle has been exploited as the basis for an extraordinary number and variety of specialized or individualistic vehicles, from the first ventures on surplus Second World War military types to out-and-out sports cars; from coachbuilt cars to the kit cars that largely supplanted those traditional types, from buggies to drag racers. Far and away the best-known descendant of the original Beetle is, of course, Porsche.

The first Porsche, built by Dr Porsche's son Ferry in 1948, was in many respects a Volkswagen special, although it did have its modified VW engine ahead of the rear axle (subsequent road Porsches through to the Seventies were closer to the Beetle, with engine behind the rear axle line). Porsche outgrew its origins, and was to outlive lapses into inbreeding, but its Volkswagen connections were not abandoned; the royalty it received on every Beetle built was valuable, and so was the R&D work for Volkswagen, while there was a direct model association in the VW-Porsche 914 of the Seventies.

Denzel came as a contemporary of Porsche, but any chance it had of emulating that company was lost as it did not progress beyond Beetle specials. Austrian Wolfgang Denzel built his first

cars on Second World War surplus Kübelwagen chassis, but is remembered for his little sports cars of the Fifties. Some had the Beetle floorpan, but a shorter chassis was normal, with Beetle suspension, engines in capacities from 1.1 to 1.5 litres, and transmission. They were available 1953-60, but failed to achieve wide popularity despite some success in local rallies, and once in a major event when Denzel-Stroinig headed the overall classification in the 1954 Alpine Rally.

Denzel did not have the benefit of the kind of association that Wilhelm Karmann eventually enjoyed with Nordhoff, neither did Friedrich Rometsch, although his sporting cabriolets were surely as deserving. Rometsch is usually remembered for stretched four-door Beetle saloons, often found serving as taxis in Germany in the Fifties. However, during the first half of that decade, this Berlin coachbuilder produced very smart two/three-seat cabriolets and coupés on the Beetle platform. These had aluminium bodies, with extended front and rear overhang which disguised the origins of the chassis and running gear. They had no pretensions to real high performance, but were boulevard cars with an air of quality that made them attractive to such personalities as film stars. A sharper Sport Kabriolett came in 1957, but few were built.

Generically, these Rometsch cars were dubbed Beeskow, for designer Johannes Beeskow who moved on to work for Karmann.

High-class bodies were also built by the Drews brothers between 1948 and 1951, most of the 150 or so being cabriolets with a hard-top option, and by Beuttler and Dannenhauer & Strauss in very small numbers. But the appearance of the Karmann-Ghias in the mid-Fifties, and the emergence of fibreglass bodies and kit cars at around the same time discouraged the 'real coachbuilders': Jensen showed just what could be done with fibreglass with its 541 in 1954, and very soon after that some of the first fibreglass bodies to be mounted on Beetle floorpans were introduced by Ascort and Proctor in Australia.

This approach to building individualistic cars on mass-production bases did not catch on in Brazil until the Seventies, and that gave Puma a chance to flourish. The first cars bearing this name came in 1964, using DKW components; VW do Brasil took over in 1967, and substituted the Beetle floorpan and engine. The stylish GTS1600 open two-seater and the GTE1600 coupé on a shortened floorpan followed. Some were exported, but fell foul of Ford's registration of the Puma name, while the next models failed to meet some regulations (for example, headlight height) in prospective markets.

The SP, introduced in 1972, used the standard floorpan and torsion bar suspension with anti-roll bars, the SP-1 having the 1.6-litre engine rated at 54 bhp, the SP-2 being a bored-out 1.7-litre 65-bhp version. The body was low and

slippery, with a well-equipped cockpit and good luggage space in the nose (where the spare wheel was ahead of the axle line). VW do Brasil claimed top speeds of 92 mph (149 km/h) and 100 mph (161 km/h).

These could be seen as Seventies equivalents of the sporty Karmann-Ghia models, and were run alongside the locally-built Karmann-Ghia TC based on the VW Type 3 (1600). They were certainly more handsome than the Osnabrück Karmann-Ghias, but international promise was undermined as VW do Brasil quite simply neglected to research market requirements and restrictions.

Puma turned to front-engine GTB models,

American trike enthusiasts have favoured easily-available and sturdy Beetle components, and this one seen on Daytona Beach went further, gaining weather protection for his machine with some Beetle bodywork. That might become detached, and one day an auto archaeologist will puzzle over the remains of a Beetle with rear fuel tank filler...

but maintained the VW link with the GTE coupé and GTS spider until 1985. Then under new ownership, it continued the Beetle-based sports car line with the AM2, which looked not unlike the Ferrari 308, and was carried on the familiar platform chassis and torsion bars suspension; with the flat four rated at 44 bhp as the Eighties ended, it gave an 87-mph (140-km/h) top speed. That was succeeded by the AM4, using the Passat engine or larger GM units. This marked the end of main-line sports cars based on the Beetle. But there were still many small-scale independent models using the base components of VW's classic which are too numerous to list – even if a definitive list were feasible.

Setting aside buggies and the practice of over-embellishing normal saloons that had its origins in California in the Sixties and became widespread, the Beetle-based 'sports' cars in 'kit' and complete turn-key forms fell into two broad categories. The first comprised cars with replacement bodies that had original lines, the

second Beetles with bodies revised to resemble well known sports cars.

Targa-top open cars and coupés, often with gull-wing doors, were favourite types among the kit manufacturers (that term flatters some, for fibreglass body kits could be produced in very modest premises). The range was limited in the Sixties but grew rapidly in the early Seventies before suffering a downturn, then returning to a healthier level that was maintained in the next decade.

Fiberfab came early to the field with the Aztec, produced for the local California market in 1965. At the time, this coupé was notable for its low lines (just over 40 in/100 cm high), rather incongruously combined with VW 15-inch wheels. A Beetle chassis, together with running gear, engine and transmission, of course, was the start point. The saloon body was discarded, the platform chassis strengthened to a degree as stiffness was lost, and the Aztec body bolted to it. Fiberfab claimed that little skill was necessary,

Boating Beetles

The surviving Schwimmwagens have a devoted following, and the Sixties seemed a good time to indulge in aquatic antics as well as an obvious way of exploiting the renowned sealing qualities of the Beetle: successful voyages were made with careful additional sealing to make cars really watertight.

Two Australians 'sailed' a VW across Sydney harbour late in the Fifties, and a first notable open sea crossing was made in 1964 when two Italians negotiated the notorious currents of the Strait of Messina between the Italian mainland and Sicily in a 1200. Other adventures, such as a trip from the Isle of Man to the British mainland followed, and there was a rash of Beetle sailings on lakes and waterways. The odd car did however sink from time to time.

In general, any holes in the bodywork (for cables, for example,) had to be fully sealed, while additional rubber door seals were normal. An electric bilge pump in the cockpit was no more than sensible. The engine needed to be waterproofed, although its compartment was not, and exhausts extended above water level. Drive was taken to a marine propeller, and steering was by the front wheels. Cars with a sun-roof seemed popular – the crew could stand, for improved visibility, and act as easily adjustable ballast – and presumably, in the event of the need arising, quickly abandon ship!

The intrepid Mal Buchanan during his voyage from the Isle of Man to the English mainland. He is obviously intent on a fast passage, and this disregard for economy may have been the reason why he ran out of fuel with a few hundred yards to go. However, the wind saw him safely to land.

the only tools needed being spanners, screwdrivers and a drill. The kit would normally include necessary components such as bulkheads, and could include complete cockpit fittings (for example, a pair of bucket seats). The cockpit top was front-hinged, with an hydraulic support, and the engine cover was hinged at the tail to give access to the spare wheel as well as the flat four. The car was slightly shorter than a Beetle, and a complete Aztec weighed in at around 1300 lb (590 kg), almost 400 lb (180 kg) less than a standard saloon.

The Aztec was cheap, and the quality of the finished car depended on the effort a buyer was prepared to put into it. Fiberfab was to move on to other kits, still using VW running gear, and included a second Aztec in imitation of the Ford GT40 that many felt inspired the company's first model. As the operation became more sophisticated, Fiberfab kits were made in Germany for a dozen years from 1971. This first Aztec is an important early example of the Beetle-based fibreglass-bodied kit car.

Since they appeared, kits and conversions have been originated in a dozen countries, with America, Australia, Brazil and Britain in the forefront, but with very few appearing in Germany and Austria, while the Philippines contributed several in the Seventies (when the Beetle was still assembled there). Great ingenuity disguised the origins of some sleek little coupés: but there were inferior cars, in terms of practicality as well as appearance, which tended to give the kit industry a dubious reputation.

The Nova stood out among first-generation special-bodied Beetles. Designed by Richard Oates, and introduced in 1971, this low coupé was notable for its lines and the fact that it was produced in Australia (the Purvis), in the United States (the Sterling), Italy and South Africa (where it was confusingly named the Puma). Its later British history was erratic, reflecting the kit industry.

The 'cottage industry' element became more apparent as designs appeared under different names. A good example was the handsome gull-wing Saluki, introduced by Siva in 1973: after Siva folded, it was produced as an Embeesa from 1977, then it became the DJ Charger early in the Eighties before being passed on to MDB to be re-

Porsche lines were followed by Dannenhauser & Strauss in the late Fifties (ABOVE), in the Chesil Speedster (OPPOSITE BELOW) of the Eighties, and in Technic's 550 Spyder of the late Eighties (OPPOSITE ABOVE). Both are Beetle based, and are high quality 'replicars'.

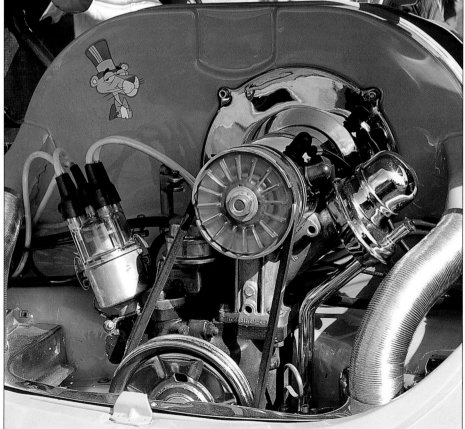

engineered for Ford components under its still striking body lines.

The Beetle floorpan and mechanical components have been of inestimable value to constructors of replicars leading to a wide variety of different creations, some rather odd, to say the least: an evocation of the Lamborghini Countach on a Beetle chassis and running gear somehow lacks conviction!

The Belgian Apal company was a pioneer in the field of original Beetle-based coupés, later turning to a good-looking copy of the early-Fifties Porsche 356 Speedster – a most appropriate car. The 356 became a popular subject, with British, German and Brazilian types, a rare French replicar (the Roadster Car), and a particularly nice Super 90 by Envemo in Brazil, credited with a 103-mph (165-km/h) top speed in its early-Eighties 1.6-litre form.

Other choices have seemed somewhat odd – 'Bugatti T35s' from Austria, France, Germany and the United States, inevitably let down by the wheelbase and track proportions of the donor Beetle; MG T replicars, including TCs from

Holland and the United States, a TD from the
United States and a TF from France; there has
been an Alfa Romeo Monza, Mercedes-Benz SS
and SSK, a Riley Kestrel and a Ford GT40 (one
of the earliest Beetle-based replicars by Ferrer, in
the United States, in the mid-Sixties).

Improving the original led to cars such as the
Nineties Burly, a coupé obviously inspired by the
Hebmüllers of the late Forties. Then there have
been evocations of street-rods of an earlier era,

for example, the Thirties Willys (the Wizard
Roadster) or flathead Ford (by BGW), that were
still obviously Beetles.

Lower lines for saloons have attracted some,
although in their appearance roof-chopped bodies
picked up an old theme (*L'Automobile* suggested
that the early-Nineties Hoffman Top-Chop had an
air d'avant guerre, as it seemed to the magazine
to follow the slit-window lines favoured by
French coachbuilders in the Thirties). Roof-

chopped Beetles first attracted attention as drag race contestants sought aerodynamic advantages, and street versions came in the Seventies – not many, perhaps, as the appeal of this particular form of beautification is essentially personal.

Personalizing is, of course, the reason for customizing and was as much at the heart of the California Beetle scene as drag racing in the quarter-century after production ended in Germany, and the two activities were always intertwined. Discretion was never part of either, and on streets – American, European or South American – custom Beetles grab attention. In southern California they supported a minor automotive sub-industry (elsewhere, efforts tended to owe more to individual efforts).

The 'California Look' went well beyond a high-quality paint scheme and the removal of most standard external components and trim (sometimes local laws meant that a form of bumper had to be retained). Lowered suspension and specialist wheels are important to looks and may enhance performance, but in most respects a hot engine is the item that really counts; usually, these cars are about show *and* go, although sometimes paint and distinctive wheels are simple enhancements for a car with a mundane mechanical specification. Internal treatment can often match the highest coachbuilding qualities, and given that, who could be satisfied with Wolfsburg's measly instrumentation?

Essentially, these have always been individual machines, so a description of any one, two, three, or more, serves little purpose. They have to be seen, shown off to fellow buffs, and where better than at a Beetle meeting. The Bug-Ins passed into legend, but there are still meets large and small, the former attracting fringe culture crowds as well as true Beetle enthusiasts. The best have been staged where full facilities for competition motoring were available (essentially a drag strip), but casual field events in a motoring tradition stretching back to pre-First World War days still hold great appeal. The supply of good, cheap, cars will probably not dry up for many years, so the Beetle seems set to run on for a long time as the most popular subject for customizing.

Its place in the buggy world is equally secure. The first amateur-built cars that came in the late Fifties, as beach buggies or dune buggies, were usually little more than Beetles stripped of all bodywork, maybe with some roll-over protection and four individual exhausts pointing skywards with no muffler to subdue their unmusical sound. The type became really popular

as off-road recreational vehicles in the Sixties, and the middle of that decade saw large meets in southern California, in territory that would have been considered Jeep country in the Fifties. Soon, the competitive element of some meets became serious and the machines progressed from the simple fun buggy concept, the serious off-road racers becoming very specialized, though most used some VW components.

The archetypal early buggy was the Meyers Manx, from 1964. B.F. Meyers was originally a boat-building company and this was reflected in the hull-like fibreglass one-piece chassis of the first Manx, reinforced with steel tubes, which also served as a very open body; roll-over protection and a skid plate to guard engine and transmission were optional extras. Beetle suspension, engine and transmission were normal, although with an extension kit a Chevrolet Corvair engine could be used. The wheelbase was only 78 inches (198 cm).

Bruce Meyers progressed to a shortened Beetle floorpan, and to fibreglass bodies with more svelte lines, especially on the street buggies of the Eighties. Meanwhile, a much tougher Manx won the first Baja race, in 1967, when Wilson and Mangels covered the 920 miles (1,470 km) of desert racing in just over 27 hours.

Meyers' buggies were successful in market terms for years. Prominent mid-Sixties competitors in Southern California included EMPI with the Sportster, which had simple angular metal bodywork on a shortened Beetle chassis, naturally with Beetle running gear and power. EMPI was a well-established and respected VW tuning and preparation company. Like the Meyers, its buggies were to become more refined, with rounded fibreglass bodywork arriving for the Seventies.

These American buggies inspired others in several countries, with constructors such as GP Vehicles becoming widely-known and originating styles rather than simply imitating them.

This was another Beetle-derived sport that led to the formation of national and local clubs and the distinctly less formal groups which often delighted in odd titles, and to the support of magazines. These testified to the strength of this Volkswagen as an enthusiast's car – an idea that can hardly have arisen at the beginning of its long and troubled gestation some 60 years earlier.

This roof-chopped Beetle is equipped for a drag strip, but here it is in a docile run-past at an enthusiasts' meet.

9. A BEETLE FOR THE 21ST CENTURY – THE NEW BEETLE

Concept I was the sensation of the Detroit Show in January 1994 when Volkswagen executives quite clearly stated that it was not the forerunner of a production model. By the next motor show, at Geneva in March 1994, the strong public reaction had led to a corporate change of mind, and chairman Ferdinand Piëch decided that it would be developed as a production model. Beetle had never been an official VW name, but the public inevitably saw Concept I as 'Beetle II', and on the Volkswagen stand at the 1996 Geneva Motor Show it was presented as 'the new Beetle'. The aim was 1998 production for sale in the United States first with models arriving in European show rooms in the autumn.

Concept I had started life as a study for an electric car, initiated at the VW-Audi California design studio under J. Mays. In 1992 it was taken up as a group project in Germany under Hartmut Warkuss, who transferred from Audi to head the VW design group at Wolfsburg.

The silhouette and styling features within it, such as the wheel arches, were strongly and deliberately reminiscent of the Beetle. The short nose and tail were by no means Beetle copies, and those wheel arches had to bulge to accommodate the thin but tall 18-inch wheels. There never was an intention to build a replicar.

In mechanical aspects the Concept cars – the first was joined by a cabriolet in time for the 1994 Geneva show – were far removed from the Beetle. In 1994 the electric model was seen as one in a range, to include versions with a 1.9-

The response to Volkswagen's yellow Concept I (BELOW) was very strong when it was shown early in 1994. The shapes were rounded, even bulbous, and the 18-inch wheels seemed large, but those echoes of the Beetle remained. Unlike many concept cars, these designs were practical, and were to lead on to the new Beetle. The New Beetle has ingenious design features, such as the sliding glass roof on this 1996 Geneva Motor Show car (LEFT). In complete contrast to the old Beetle, its engine is in the nose and drives the front wheels (INSET).

Specification
New Beetle

Wheelbase:	*99 in/251 cm*
Overall length:	*160 in/406 cm*
Overall width:	*68 in/173 cm*
Overall height:	*59.5 in/151 cm*

drive to come). Initially, the new Beetle was to be offered with the direct fuel injection turbo-diesel or the petrol engines. The former was expected to give it a top speed of around 180 km/h (112 mph).

Development from design study to prototype involved many detail changes, but the unique shape was broadly unchanged. Most noticeably, bumper protrusions were styled into the rear. Seemingly, the new Beetle was not outstanding in aerodynamic respects, with VW claiming no more than a drag coefficient of 'below 0.40'. Neither was it a small car, in terms of the mid-Nineties or compared with the classic Beetle of some 20 years earlier:

In some dimensions, notably wheelbase and width, the 1996 new Beetle is a little larger than Concept I, and that could only benefit interior space. This is already more generous than the classic Beetle's in every respect except rear-seat headroom.

The interior of the show cars was also much brighter – the fascia perhaps too bright and more appropriate to some of the mid-Nineties retro-cars (the new Beetle is decidedly not among these). In a Beetle tradition there is one large, round instrument, ahead of the driver in a modest binnacle and combining speedometer and water temperature and fuel gauges. From Concept I there is provision for air conditioning, and a radio occupies the centre of the fascia. The rear seats can be folded to increase luggage space.

All-round visibility is excellent, and the car at the Geneva show in 1996 had a Porsche-system glass roof which slid back and down over the large rear window to give an open top (a fabric blind subdued sunlight or street-light distractions). Anti-lock brakes were specified, and safety equipment includes twin air bags and side air bags.

A new factory, alongside VW's Puebla plant in Mexico, was commissioned to build the new Beetle (amazingly, the original type was still in production). The U.S. market was the prime target, and early indications were that the new Beetle would be seen as a new car, rather than as a modern car with old body lines, while the association with the classic Beetle would bring unquestioned advantages.

It is safe to predict that sales will never match the staggering Beetle totals, but there is little doubt that its successor will secure a positive place in the markets from 1998 and on into the 21st century.

litre turbo-diesel and hybrid diesel/electric power. Later, two petrol versions with 105-bhp and 150-bhp power units were added to the programme. These were in-line engines, for transverse installation, and drove the front wheels (with the option of syncro four-wheel-

LEFT

Two years after Concept I appeared the transition to a production car was almost complete, as the new Beetle was exhibited. There were many detail changes – some can be seen in this shot, which compares with the Concept I three-quarter front view on page 77 – but the essential style was retained.

INSET

The cockpit appears comfortable and roomy and provides good visibility through the large glass areas. In Beetle tradition there is just one multi-function instrument, ahead of the driver and possibly partly obscured by the air-bag housing. The passenger grab handle also echoes some earlier Beetles. The radio is a standard fitting, and incidental stowage space seems adequate.

INDEX